THE 5 STAR POINTS FOR SUCCESS

Manifest Your Dreams
Live Your Life's Purpose

JACQUELINE OYA THOMAS, M.A.

SPIRIT OF OYA

Published by Spirit of Oya

P.O. BOX 10064
Marina Del Rey CA 90295

Editor: Julia Rogers
Illustrator: Steven Lopez
Author photo courtesy of Carlos Armando

The 5 Star Points for Success
Manifest Your Dreams
Live Your Life's Purpose

ISBN
978-0-99098-020-9 (print)
978-0-9909-021-6 (ebook)

Printed in the United States of America

Website: www.spiritofoya.com
Email: hello@spiritofoya.com

Gratitude to ...

The spirit of my Father, Ezekiel. Thank you for assisting me in becoming the woman and artist that I have become.

The spirit of my Grandmother, Rosie. Thank you for helping me reconnect with my inner child and my spirit.

The spirit of my Economics teacher, Mr. Mitzenberg. Thank you for nurturing my entrepreneurial spirit.

My mother, Annie. Thank you for your heartfelt involvement in my life and for teaching me about the most important qualities in life.

My brother, Patrick. Thank you for allowing me to share my ideas and for supporting all of my dreams.

All of my Rays of Light. Thank you for your support, encouragement and for believing in me.

Thank you, from the bottom of my heart!

TABLE OF CONTENTS

INTRODUCTION

to The 5 Star Points for Success:
Manifest Your Dreams, Live Your Life's Purpose

Hello, my lovely and amazing creators! First of all, I am so glad you're here. And also, congratulations! If you are reading this, it means you are a creative, imaginative, special person who has made the decision to finally take the necessary steps to pursue what is deep within you – to manifest your dreams and live your life's purpose.

This book is all about *you*. That's right: YOU! I wrote this spiritual life guide to help *you* tap into your heart's needs. Certainly, other people will always have opinions about the way you should live your life, and many will come and go. But now is the time to be with *yourself* and honor your belief that you can be the person you've always wanted to be and make the most of your time on this earth.

I devised my "5 Star Points for Success" system to help anyone with a creative mind build a rock-solid foundation for living an exceptional life grounded in the five core components of self: **MIND; BODY; SPIRIT; EMOTIONS and ENVIRONMENT**. I have arrived at this system through my lifelong study of human spirituality and the Arts and through my own journey and now I want to share it with you – to show you how I tapped into my own harmony using this system and inspire you to dive head first into your own divine power. I want you to take pure delight in every day and connect with your authentic self so you can lead a fulfilling life, totally energized by your wildest dreams.

So many people get caught up in everyday living, in paying bills and in just barely "going through the motions" that they don't stop to think about what they want their lives to be, how they feel or what is going on around them. They work every single day, Monday through Friday, get home just in time to (maybe) make some dinner and unwind for just a few moments, only to go to bed, get up and do it all over again the next day.

Do you relate to this kind of life? If you do, by the time the weekend comes, you may or may not enjoy the time off, because not only are you physically drained, but you are also mentally, emotionally, and even spiritually depleted, possibly also living in a cluttered home that does not support or refresh you. Suddenly, it's Sunday night already and time for another exhausting week to start.

Some people use their work to prove their worth, but are not happy. How would it feel to be doing what you love and being you, in all your glory? I can tell you, because I am living it: It would feel amazing! Reading this book is your opportunity to get on that path and start fresh, so you better get while the getting's good!

Do you love drama? Well, cut that out!
Sometimes our lives can be so filled with drama that we cannot even think straight. We go into survival mode, and then we are too zapped to even think about doing anything creative or focusing on our own happiness. You can use the information in this book to help you face those ugly monsters, those little and big dramas that are happening inside and all around us, so you can eliminate them from your life, move forward, and fulfill your true purpose with joy.

The process of cutting out the drama can get sticky for so many people, because they just do not want to deal with it. But cutting out the drama is where you need to start in order to get ahead. Think about it this way: If you are distracted by drama ...

How can you create?

How can you focus on yourself if you are constantly worried about your significant other, arguing with others, fixated on paying bills, your health or anything else that is disturbing your peace?

You just cannot. That is why you have to clear out the clutter, inside and out!

You cannot start doing anything with a shaky foundation, which is why the 5 Star Points system is so important. This system is all about turning yourself into a strong and impenetrable fortress that cannot be moved, even when drama enters your life. The Big Bad Wolf will not be able to huff, puff, or blow your powerful brick house down. No gusty, dramatic winds will be able to harm you, and no rain will drown you in a torrential flood, because you will have taken the time to work on you and stand tall, proud, and unshakeable, focused on your goals.

Time is of the essence, and you do not need to waste a single moment on silly nonsense that does not contribute to fulfilling your destiny. Every minute you waste is a minute you could be spending creating exactly what you want in your life. Why waste valuable breath and time on drama and any hullabaloo that is not heart-centered and contributing to forward momentum?

The Time for the 5 Star Points is NOW!
I truly want to help you raise your level of consciousness, so you can clear away the clutter, find your own authenticity, accept yourself for the person you are and shine your inner light, regardless of your chosen professional field or your personal goals. It is my sincere hope that by following the 5 Star Points system that I will outline in the coming chapters, and by putting in the work through exercises and real-world action steps, you will fall in love with your true self, begin to honor that self, and start to embrace the fact that you can do anything. And, believe you me, when you are operating from that place of harmony and love, your glow will be contagious. You will set the world on fire!

Most importantly, you will feel the love and flow in your own home, with your family and friends, at work ... anywhere you go. Your life will seem to come to you effortlessly, because you will be in your flow, living your life's purpose fully. You will also be an inspiration for someone else to shine their light and make the world a brighter place. When you get in touch with your mind, body, spirit, emotions and environment, you will feel whole, happy, peaceful and joyous.

This system underpins everything I share with others when I am teaching them how to take pure delight in every day and lead fulfilling lives. It is by embracing this system and passing on what I believe to be the five core elements of self – MIND, BODY, SPIRIT, EMOTIONS, ENVIRONMENT – that I have been able to tap into the vibrations of my own harmony and show others how to build a foundation that will help them manifest their dreams.

It really is all about harmony! We all need to take care of ourselves and our spirits, so we can thrive and live fully. I have seen amazing transformations in people as they feed the 5 Star Points every day: They begin to truly shine like the stars they are and make a beautiful impact on the world.

In the following chapters, we will explore each of the 5 Star Points in depth, and you will hear some inspiring stories about how I and others have found paths towards our true calling. I will also be giving you some exercises to do to help you find a new, positive way of thinking about yourself and get you in touch with your inner zest.

But first, let me give you a little taste of the 5 Star Points, so you can get a better understanding of the core concepts we will be diving into throughout this book.

"Why do I need to pay attention to the 5 Star Points?"

If you are asking yourself some version of the above question right now, listen up! I'm going to give you some quick points to think about when it comes to your mind-body-spirit-emotions-environment connection, and how it can lead to a gratifying life:

If you hate how you look and feel to your core, and allow your **MIND** to feed these negative thoughts all day, you will be surging with toxicity. How will you live with total gusto and be your genuine self through all this unproductive mental energy?

★ You cannot eat junk food all day thinking you are feeding your **BODY** the energy it needs to do great things. If your body feels terrible, how can you move forward and empower your dreams?

★ You can go to church, temple or meditate once per week ... but will this hour or two provide you with a long-lasting connection to your **SPIRIT**? You might leave the experience each week feeling full, but then a few days later, if you are not grounded, negative judgments about yourself and others can begin to creep in and try to steal your light.

★ Maybe you believe you are sensitive, in touch with your own **EMOTIONS** and the feelings of others and able to use this compassion to connect and create a positive vibe around you. But if in reality, you are an emotional wreck, how will you be able to accomplish the wonderful things that will make you and your loved ones happy?

★ You might spend most of your day out in the world doing what you love and making a positive impact on the world. But if you come home to a chaotic and dissatisfying **ENVIRONMENT** every night, how can you expect to feel well balanced and stress free?

Do not despair! The 5 Star Points system has your back!

If we want everything around us and within us to flow, each of us must be in alignment. Below is an introduction to the core of the different components of my "5 Star Points for Success" system. As you absorb these, think about how these different pieces of "self" fit into your daily experiences. Let these be the first bricks of your own foundation, so you can start to come into your own light and start a new, upbeat vibration. And remember: You have to rock before you roll!

Your Amazing *MIND*

The power of our mind is miraculous. What we feed our mind, what we allow to take root and grow creates either healthy or unhealthy thoughts that can either support us or hinder us. The mind can either push us through the tough times or keep us mired in them.

Is your mind sending you positive messages or negative messages?

Are you telling yourself, "I'm amazing and worthy" or are you thinking, "I am a bad person and do not deserve success and happiness?"

When going gets tough, do you fight tooth and nail to cross the threshold or do you give up?

Try this experiment: Take a moment and think about a goal – either short term or long term – that you have for your life. Now, think about that goal in two different ways:

1. "Oh, I could never do that. That's too hard. It will never happen."

How does that thought make you feel?

2. Envision that same goal along with all your talents, all the gifts you can offer to the world, everything that makes you unique as a human being and say, "YES, I CAN DO IT." Say it out loud and feel the power of what your mind can do when you think positively.

So many people do not understand the implications of how and what they are thinking, and when they delve deeper into their minds, they are stunned by all the negative thoughts and judgments. Are the negative stories you are telling yourself actually true? Most of the time, the answer is, "No." You are just operating from a low vibration – an old, sad story you just can't seem to shake. When you have destructive thoughts, you have just moved so far away from your authentic self that you just need some realignment and a new "business plan" for your life. (More about that in Chapter 1!)

We can all rewrite our story by visualizing it with our minds – by using positive intentions and affirmations as tools to ground our dreams. I have watched people that initially thought their dreams were ridiculous bring them to fruition. All they had to do was believe.

So, when you start feeling that negativity creep into your mind … kick it out! And don't be nice about it – kick hard! Take control of those thoughts … and then turn them around. Think, shout, scream from the rooftops, "I CAN DO IT!!!" And you know what? YOU WILL!

Your Powerful BODY
The body is the temple of our soul and where our spirit resides. If we take good care of our body, our spirit thrives. If we fail to nourish, maintain, and energize our body, our soul can grow weary.

How can you live out your dreams when you are unhealthy and worn down?

Many people do not realize how critical their physical health is to their spiritual, mental and emotional health, nor do they realize that how they feel physically can actually affect their environment, and all people, places, and things within it.

I have a few questions about your body:

★ Are you eating healthily and well?

★ On any given day, do you feel stagnant, or does energy flow through your body, to the point where you feel compelled to keep moving?

★ Do you get sick frequently and feel tired all the time?

★ When you look at yourself in the mirror, are you happy with what you see?

If you are depriving or abusing the body your spirit needs to function, you will have a difficult time feeling full and empowered. If you feel exhausted, depleted and ill all the time, you will not be able to live your dream. While it sounds simple, resting, drinking plenty of water, eating right and exercising regularly can mean the difference between being capable, excited, and alive and struggling to accomplish even the most basic daily tasks you need to survive.

When I meet people who are not living their heart's purpose, they often tell me how low their energy levels are; "I just don't feel like it," or "I'm just too exhausted" are their regular refrains. But I've also watched these people change their habits, start taking care of themselves and suddenly have the oomph they need to take action steps to create more joy and purpose in their lives.

The body can deeply affect what we can accomplish. You need it to fuel your mind, spirit and emotions as you move fluidly through your environment. If you are smoking or drinking excessively, or engaging in other negative behaviors that actively go against nurturing and supporting your body, you will not be able to move forward. Take responsibility for your body, because, without it, you will be unable to shine your light to its full capacity.

Your Indomitable *SPIRIT*

Our spirit is our intuition, love, radiance, creative juices, and the strength that is within us to do great, prosperous things. As little children, we are deeply in touch with this spirit. It is who we are at our core, and it drives us to dream and share these dreams with others. It makes us believe anything is possible.

Many of us lose contact with our spirits as we get older, because we get overwhelmed by our busy lives and forget to connect to ourselves, listen to our inner voices, and feel ... or perhaps we disconnected because someone told us our dreams were silly or impossible and would not amount to anything. Still, we hear incredible stories all the time about people whose spirits have empowered their bodies and allowed them to surmount huge challenges in ways that are almost inexplicable. Knowing this magic can happen, why oh why would we want to disconnect?

Take a moment to check in with yourself.

★ Are you present and accounted for, actually inside your own body, feeling good about who you are?

★ Are you living your life authentically?

★ Is your spirit's light dim ... or are you shining bright?

There are many people out there who live a lie because they let themselves pretend to be somebody they are not instead of proudly standing up for who they are. They lose touch with their spirit's voice: that little child they once were, capable of clearly articulating the dreams their spirit was here to accomplish. Instead of encouraging these wonderful individuals to accept themselves fully and shine their lights, the voice says they are not worthy of living a joyous life. When you embrace your spirit fully, your inner voice will say, "You are worthy," and you will be able to reconnect with yourself and with others to co-create a magnificent world where magical experiences take place.

The concept of "co-creation" is confusing to many, because they are so far away from their authentic spirit. And even when they understand the concept, they cannot map out the road back. But once you live fully and operate from the source of love, acceptance and dreams within you, you will find the strength to accomplish amazing things.

Your Electrifying *EMOTIONS*

Repeat after me: "Emotions are my friends."

So many people get "weirded out" by emotions, because having them is so often seen as a human weakness. We are surrounded by people who, when we express our feelings, regularly tell us, "Stop being so emotional" or "You are too emotional."

But guess what? To be human is to feel! And our emotions can teach us so much about ourselves. When we are free of negative thoughts or judgments, emotions are natural and authentic evaluations of what is happening deep within our souls. They are a window to our inner truth, and we need to be encouraged to stay connected to them and to express them to others.

In order to stay connected to yourself and everything in your environment, I encourage you to regularly ask yourself whether you are satisfied or dissatisfied, happy or sad. Then ask, "Why?" Riding the emotional roller coaster can actually be a positive, healthy experience that can help you understand what is at work all around you so you can make decisions and cultivate wonderful events in your life.

I have personally gone against my emotions before and learned some difficult yet valuable lessons about mistrusting the vibrations my heart is sending me. Now, when I am experiencing something, and I get a yummy emotional feeling that brings me almost to tears, I instantly connect with the feeling that I am in a genuine, loving space of gratitude. And then I know wherever I am is where I need to be at that exact time. And when I am in a situation where my gut instinct says, "This is not right," I know I need to get out of that situation immediately.

Instead of feeling overwhelmed by your emotions, see them as your allies in your ongoing quest to live the life you've always dreamed of living. People make some of their best decisions from a grounded, centered place overflowing with true feelings. When we reach out and touch these emotions, we can ride the truth wave to an honesty and openness with ourselves that will help us shine our special lights in the world.

Your Peaceful *ENVIRONMENT*

What we see and what goes on outside us are outer manifestations of what is going on inside us. All the environments we encounter – the environments we travel to in the outside world, the environment we create within our homes and within our bodies and minds – are inter-connected. And our ability to create peace and harmony in all these environments is critical.

My passion for observing life, my spiritual psychology degree, and my work as a certified feng shui practitioner have always driven me to explore how we interact with our environment. What I have learned is that you need to create a home that supports you and your dreams. In my own home, I surround myself with both things that will ground me and things that will set me on fire.

You can learn a lot about the spaces in which you are dwelling by being inquisitive about the people, places, and things you encounter every day:

How do you live, and what is the energy of those with whom you live?

What do you have in your home, and do these "things" support the dream you want to live ... or do they remind you of negative memories that are hindering your growth?

What are you watching every day on television, and do these programs lift or lower your vibration?

You need to create a flow of fresh energy that circulates in all areas of your life, from career, to your romantic relationships, to your children and your quest towards wealth, happiness and prosperity. You need to explore all the rooms of your world and your soul and figure out how to create harmony within them if you want to build the solid foundation for a life well lived, because, choosing to live well now will inspire living well in the future.

When you start to tune into these 5 Star Points for Success, you will find a foundation that will support the exceptional life you want to lead. You will fall in love with yourself – your true self, begin to honor that self and start to believe you can do anything. And when you are operating from a place of harmony and love, others will see you glowing – from states and even countries away.

You will feel the love and flow in your own home, with your family and friends, at work ... anywhere you are. Things will come to you gracefully, because you will be in your flow, living your life's purpose fully and an inspiration for someone else to shine their light and make the world a brighter place. When you get in touch with your mind, body, spirit, emotions, and environment, you will be solid, happy, peaceful and joyous.

Embodying the 5 Star Points for Success system goes far beyond "success;" it is about raising your level of consciousness, so you can clear away the clutter, find your own authenticity and accept yourself for the person you are.

Is there room in your environment for that item, person/relationship, project, career, or child that you long for but can't seem to manifest?

While purging is often essential to letting in all the love we crave, we need to take a good look at what we have, clear out what we don't need and invite in what we want with open arms. But in order to do this, we need to be ready, so that special thing we want will not just become more clutter.

You need to get rid of the mess in order to Do You and Be You – the star that you already are! And once you recognize you are a star, you can fill the sky with your light and live your dream.

> **WARNING: If you are looking for a quick fix or a band-aid to put on your life's boo-boos, you are probably not in the right place! For many, my system is a total mindset shift that is not for the faint of heart!**

Reading The 5 Star Points for Success: Manifest Your Dreams, Live Your Life's Purpose is an opportunity to make your spirit soar. Know that you are a spiritual being having a human experience. You get the precious gift of being able to utilize your spiritual gifts through your human life right here and now, so go for it! Give yourself permission to have faith, believe in yourself, and surrender to your spirit, and who you are. No matter where you are or what you are doing today, in just a matter of months, you can change your life.

How do I know?

Everything I have set out to do, from my first business in high school, to all the conferences I have spoken at as an expert, to my heartfelt success, the *Spirit of Oya* CD, I accomplished after I stopped making excuses and committed to making my dreams come true by following the principles of The 5 Star Points. I set my intention to do it, and in many cases, in just one month or less, my life began to change. I have evolved through life lessons, business lessons, experience, and education, and by constantly listening to my mind-body-spirit-emotions-environment connection. And it is this evolution that allows me to talk to others and even write this book! The proof that I can do it has been reinforced every day, as an overflow of clients asked me to perform for them and share my musical gifts and guide them through improving their own lives as they transform their careers, businesses, relationships with others and attitudes about themselves.

Now, do you want to keep making excuses, or do you want to bravely move forward and live your own dream? Maybe you think you are too old, too tired or that you just can't do it anymore, but I am here to tell you, it is never too late. That being said, you *cannot* let another second pass by.

It's time for a self-interrogation!
  ★ "What is my dream?"
  ★ "What will happen if I manifest my dream, and really go for it?"
  ★ "How do I want others to see me?"
  ★ "How will everything change if I finally allow my dream to come true?"

You need to get real with yourself before you get into the meat and potatoes of this book. Sometimes, as much as we want to pursue we can be resistant to making a life shift, because we are concerned about the outcome. As an example, we might worry that if we follow our dream, our boyfriend, girlfriend or partner may not support us; we think we will lose this person forever. Maybe your partner wants you to stay home and not travel ... or maybe it has nothing to do with your partner, and you are just afraid of leaving home because you are so comfortable where you are that you do not want to set your wheels in motion, especially if these wheels will carry you to New York City, Los Angeles, or somewhere other than where you are.

Regardless of what is stopping you and worrying you, start thinking about what you will gain from allowing your dream to come alive.

Are you creative, but find yourself unable to get anything done? Do you have projects hanging out there and starting and stopping, ideas that you keep talking about that never come to fruition? The more projects you have in motion at once, the more scattered your energy will be, and the more you will start to feel that you will never get anything done – sabotage! Your life will be full of incomplete actions, and your overwhelmed psyche will tell you it is okay not to finish; year after year, you will come up empty.

Some projects take less energy than others. Other projects will take all your attention ... and even take you to what feels like the brink of insanity! I want you to complete your projects and win. Because, when you win, you are completely changing your thought process. You are telling yourself, "I finish things! I am successful, and I can do it!" You are taking care of business, taking the bull by the horns, preventing yourself from having too many "should've, would've, could've"s floating around in your atmosphere. And every time you finish what you started, you are making completing your next project with confidence that much easier. You already know you can do it!

Case in point: The fact that I completed my CD has given me the confidence to write this book, and it has strengthened my resolve to move onto my next album. Why? Because I know I have accomplished something huge, and those accomplishments are a part of me now. I know I can do it; I have bona fide proof!

Have faith! The exercises at the end of each chapter will help activate your brain, body, and spirit and help you start to welcome the 5 Star Points system as a way to renovate your life and finish fulfilling projects with ease and grace. They will help you get into the groove and manifest thoughts of power and success.

And now, here's the one, true key for really "working it" with the exercises. My book is going to call you to task with some end-of-chapter exercises. I am going to ask you to step up, participate, and get cozy with some new ways of thinking about yourself. Some of these exercises will be fun, some will be challenging, and some will be on-going ... but all will help bring you closer to becoming the absolute star I know you can be, using your talents so you can step into your full brilliance.

(No matter what, do not feel overwhelmed! You've totally got this!)

That being said, here is the one tried-and-true tip that will help you make it or break it as you live, breathe, eat, sleep, and dream the 5 Star Points as a system for starting all your creative projects and seeing them through to their happy end:

Write it down.
Yes, it can be that simple! I am a firm believer in writing down (or typing out) to-do lists. We cannot have 101 items flying through our heads, distracting us, making us spin. When we "write it down," we can see exactly what we need to do and we feel accomplished every time we cross something off the list. We can say a hearty, "Congratulations," pat ourselves on the back, and move onto the next item.

When you complete something – even if it is just one tiny item on a to-do list – that action alone has an enormous effect: It creates a shift in your brain that makes you feel more confident and able to tackle the next task. On the flip side, every time you say you are going to do something and do not, you are actually eroding your own self-esteem. And who wants that? Write down what you need to do, praise yourself for every little victory, and then move on to greater and greater things!

Each time you "write it down," you are encouraging yourself to keep promises to you – to keep your word to yourself and really follow through, make the effort to succeed. After all, if you never take the steps to do anything, you will not succeed at doing anything.

Warm-up Exercise #1

Without further ado, here is a little exercise to get you in the 5 Star Points system mindset!

★ *Write your own to-do list.*

Write a list of things you need to get done ... and really get them done. You can start small if you need to!

Write down that email you never sent, repairing that watch that's been broken for months or years, finally gifting that television to your aunt (the one you've been promising to bring over to her house for months), or that giving your cousin that bike you never use.

If you want to think even bigger, write down some of the elements that are not working in your environment or the preoccupations that are taking up space within you, or what you need to do in order to finally get that business or project off the ground.

Whatever is on your mind, go write it down ... and then do it!

Warm-up Exercise #2: How is your Mind-Body-Spirit-Emotions-Environment connection right now?

Before you read the rest of this book, I want you to take a moment to check in with yourself. (Do not skip this part: There will be a quiz later!)

Now that you have an overview of the inextricable link between your MIND, BODY, SPIRIT, EMOTIONS, and ENVIRONMENT ...

★ *On a scale of 1 to 5 (with 5 being the highest), how would you rate your mind-body-spirit-emotions-environment connection?*

Is your MIND empowering you, or is it regularly saying, "I can't," "I won't," or "I'll never"?

Are you keeping your BODY feeling good and like a well-oiled machine that carries you through your days, or are you perpetuating unhealthy habits like excessive drinking, smoking, and not eating properly?

Does your SPIRIT feel full of intuition, love, radiance, and creativity that allows you to prosper, or does it feel tired, broken and in need of a tune-up?

Are your EMOTIONS in check and making you feel fully connected to the excitement of life, or are they overwhelming you, weighing you down, and creating a tornado inside you?

Is your ENVIRONMENT pristine, comfortable, bright, and fueling your creative efforts, or is it a cluttered, negative space, full of heavy darkness?

How do you rate? Don't forget to write it down! We will be revisiting this exercise a little bit later.

Now, let's get going on our journey together!

CHAPTER 1

Your Mission, Purpose and Intentions

Before we get into the nitty-gritty details of the different 5 Star Points, we need to have a heart-to-heart about some critical cornerstones of your foundation: your mission, purpose and intentions.

Everyone who runs a business needs a plan, a mission, purpose and intentions in order to stay on task. And if you are looking to manifest your dreams and live your life's purpose – even if you do not actually intend to start an official "business" – you are an entrepreneur whose "business" is *you* and the achievement of your goals. *You* are, in fact your most important business and your best asset.

I often check in with my own mission and purpose, especially when a situation crops up that makes me feel confused or uncertain. This process of revisiting my mission and purpose reminds me of what I am supposed to be doing and helps me figure out whether I should seize an opportunity or let it go because it is not fueling my purpose and boosting my mind-body-spirit-emotions-environment connection.

The Creative Dilemma

As a creative, you know we can often be incredibly talented in so many different areas, and that leads us to attempt to do so much that we spread ourselves thin. I'll admit I have never fully bought into the "jack of all trades" concept. While you should never let *anyone* tell you can't do several things well, I think you do have to focus on one, two, or three things (tops!) in order to really excel at them. As I have often said to myself and my clients, "You have to give those babies the attention they need to be the best they can and have the energy to nurture them so they can get what they need to grow and blossom."

Here is a truth (and a dilemma!):

You are one person.
You can only do so much, no matter how powerful and fantastic you are. And what you give to and get from the universe all has to start from within you.

If you take a look into the careers of celebrities who are thriving, you will find that while they have many talents, they have chosen to focus on just one, two or three of them, especially before their careers really started to soar. They worked on one forte tirelessly until it was established enough to stand on its own and then explored their other ideas. Even a superstar like Beyoncé first worked on becoming an in-demand singer and performer before she branched out into acting and fashion. And, of course, while Beyoncé and other celebrities of that caliber have the benefit of a team of people who help them keep building, they still had to start from the ground, up, being patient and letting one success lead to another in due time.

Become an expert in your field.
In order to really build a financially lucrative and personally-fulfilling life around doing something that feeds your soul, you need to become an expert in your field, then continue to build on that foundation. It is hard for many of us to accept the idea that we cannot be everything to everyone, but it is the truth! How you can give yourself the space and love to be true to yourself when you are scrambling to accomplish 20 things in one year? That feat is just not possible! Plus, others feel drawn to collaborate with those who have a specialty; they like focus and expertise, and are turned off by those who don't seem to have it all together because they are trying to do too many things at once.

Trust me, I am the first person to tell you that you can have everything you ever dreamed of … and then some! I am a proud dreamer! But I am also the realistic executive producer that understands time and money

... and the coach who wants you to win ... and the spiritual being who wants to nurture you so you can bloom into a beautiful flower.

Be a fully-engaged dreamer.

The term "dreamer" often gets a bad rap. We think of a dreamer as someone with his/her head in the clouds, not grounded in reality. But you can be a dreamer and still be ready, willing, and able to take the action steps to get exactly what you want from every experience.

A "fully-engaged dreamer" is able to turn wishes into real forward momentum, manifest his/her dream, stay in flow, and keep it growing to live that dream and his/her life's purpose!

If you want to set yourself up for a joy-filled life spent doing exactly what you want to do, you need to put a manageable amount on your proverbial plate. Take the time to nurture your product, project or service so it can grow the legs to stand on its own, and then begin developing the next project once the first one has spread its wings and taken flight.

There are not many artists out there that have a natural aptitude for the business side of their careers. And most of us will not have the money available up front to have a management team and tons of support. I have found success and joy in my field because I have been systematic with building my career. I have built a bridge to help me walk across that big chasm between where I started out and where I am going: that beautiful place on the other side where I am fulfilling my heart's purpose and living my dream!

FAITH

MY CURRENT STATE OF BEING

SUCCESS

FAILURE

SPIRIT OF OYA

In order to achieve your dreams, you need to take a moment, slow down and get into a business mindset. If you approach your projects and your life this way, you will bring in more work, money, prestige, respect and personal satisfaction. Your cup will overflow!

"Can I hit the reset button?"

Sometimes we just need to take time out of our busy days and take a long, hard look at our lives. We need to see what is going on and what we are doing to prevent ourselves from living in a positive state. Many people do not give themselves permission to hit the "reset" button. They see that their mission, purpose, and intentions are all flawed, but they believe it is too late to change. If you've ever felt like you just want to hit a reset button, I am here to tell you, you can.

I have heard friends and clients talk about the idea of the "reset button" after a breakup or divorce, after the loss of a parent, or the loss of a job. There is nothing wrong with hitting that button. But if you do, you need to make sure you are prepared to look closely at which elements of your life you want to change and at the parts of your life you want to keep close to you. You can create a whole new mission that can leave you feeling truly alive!

You must be prepared to build a foundation and develop a strong base, so you can live your life fully and confidently hit "reset" when the time is right is what the 5 Star Points system is really about. It is the absolute alignment of mind, body, spirit, emotions and your environment, and thus the ability to listen to what your life is telling you and understand your needs and the needs of others when you hit crossroads and places where you must change direction during your journey.

Keep Your Mind on Your Mission!

As you are starting on your journey to manifest your dreams and live your life's purpose, you need to define your mission – to be clear about who you are and what you are doing. Every successful company starts with a mission and a purpose that grows into a huge enterprise, and as individuals we are no different.

To start determining your basic mission, ask yourself, "What do I do, and who do I do it for?"

And while you're at it ...

Define your purpose and intentions.

Here are some dictionary definitions for "purpose" and "intention." While each definition is slightly different, I believe they all resonate in their own way with what you must understand in order to come up with your own plan of attack for figuring out how to manifest your dreams so you can live out your heart's purpose!

★ **pur•pose** *noun*

: the reason why something is done or used : the aim or intention of something.
: the feeling of being determined to do or achieve something.
: the aim or goal of a person : what a person is trying to do, become, etc.

: determination; resoluteness.

★ **in•ten•tion** *noun*

: the thing that you plan to do or achieve : an aim or purpose
: a determination to act in a certain way : resolve
: what one intends to do or bring about
: a concept considered as the product of attention directed to an object of knowledge

To define your *own* **purpose**, ask yourself why your service or project exists. Why do you do what you do?

To get crystal clear about your own **intentions**, consider what it is you truly want from your life. What magic do you want to make happen?

Having a purpose and intentions helps you direct your energy so you can take the proper action steps and make the best choices to make your dreams a reality, which, in turn, helps you formulate your direction. Be positive and have a specific end result in mind. For instance, my intention when I set out to gracefully write this book that you are reading right now was to share what I have learned through my self-created 5 Star Points for Success system in order to help people manifest their dreams and live their life's purpose.

What do *you* want to achieve? Do not limit yourself! Be open to the greater good and get ready to be good and surprised at what you can receive when you put all your good vibrations out there!

Break through the overwhelm!
Defining your mission, purpose and intentions and living them with gusto will help open you up to the fact that you can rise to the occasion and climb to higher and higher levels to achieve more than you may have ever thought possible. But it can also lead to overthinking that can dangerously disconnect your head from your heart.

Sometimes we all need to stop thinking so much. But that is easier said than done, and getting overwhelmed can happen to the best of us. Still, we have to listen to what our heart is telling us so we can use

---

our minds in a productive way to follow through with the action steps needed to create the life we want for ourselves!

I want to let you in on a little secret (and you might not believe me when I tell you this!): *Being overwhelmed is a choice.*

You can freak out over system overload, or you can be willing to motivate, move mountains, and make dreams happen, because dreams are what pull us into our future and away from the stories of our past. Memories are wonderful, and they help make us who we are, but be careful they do not hold you back.

Mission, Purpose and Intentions, Together at Last!
Your mission, purpose and intentions are all integral to taking good care of yourself and making sure you are authentic to your MIND, BODY, SPIRIT, EMOTIONS and ENVIRONMENT. They help you create a laser-focused vision that allows you to stay committed through the challenges you will face. These foundational elements allow you to co-create with heartfelt purpose and to develop the trust necessary to take the leaps of faith needed to get up and at 'em with your goals and stay on task.

I believe that identifying your mission, purpose and intentions is mandatory for anyone providing a creative service, just as it is necessary for any successful company. Every one of us should have one so we are totally clear on what is at the root of our dreams. And of course, when you are clear, your customer will also be clear.

Having a mission, purpose and intentions also keeps you on track so you can keep moving forward on your path. If you are ever confused or are approached to do something that makes you feel uncomfortable because you are concerned it is outside your area of expertise, you can always compare it against your well-thought-out mission and purpose, so you are not distracted by opportunities that do not align with your heart-centered life.

When you know who you are, and your clients know who you are, you shine a clear light that will attract the exact people you want it to attract. You will energetically pull the proper people into your orbit, and they will see you and get you. This allows you to continue to hone your offering to attract clients who will truly value you, so you can earn what you are worth, and co-create with the best of the best! If you want to go for your dreams and create your best work, follow through and throw yourself into every project with all you have. People will remember you, re-hire you again and again and spread the word about how wonderful you are, so you can keep living your dream!

You are marvelous, so why would you settle for anything less than the whole enchilada?

Mission, Purpose, and Intention Exercise #1: Your Intentions

★ *Formulate your intentions.*

Think about what you want to achieve, and write down your intentions. The sky's the limit, so think big! Be open to the universe and the possibilities it can bring.

Setting intentions is a fabulous skill to learn, and you will be refining your intentions regularly as you continue to work on strengthening your mind-body-spirit-emotions-environment connection and watch your world expand.

If you are not sure where to start when developing your intention, follow these tips!

1. Start your intention with the phrase "MY INTENTION IS."
2. Be clear and to the point about what you want so your outcome can be equally definite.
3. Keep all language positive, so you can tell your mind and spirit that negative energy is not welcome here!
4. Allow yourself to channel the messages from your heart, and do not escape into the vast space of your own ego.

Mission, Purpose, and Intention Exercise #2:
Affirmations about Your Best Qualities

Throughout this book, I will be asking you to come up with some affirmations to keep you on target with your goals. Affirmations help us secure our positive thoughts and anchor our mission, purpose and intentions firmly to the ground. They help reprogram our minds and hearts to believe in what we want to materialize and work towards our dreams every day, so we can focus on our strengths and take our action steps with enthusiasm. An affirmation sometimes starts as a wish, but by saying it out loud and repeating it to yourself over and over again, you can make it a reality!

> ★ *With your intentions in mind, create an affirmation that declares you want you and the project or business you are working on to be the very best they can be.*

Feeling lost? Here are a couple tips for creating positive, yummy affirmations that allow you to see all you have going for you, and that you are capable of absolutely anything!

1. Meditate on your best qualities and on what really gets you revved up.
2. Think about tangible ways you want to be better and how your life can improve. What is something you feel will ground you and make you feel rock solid in your life and business (for example, more peace, joy, harmony around and inside you, more self-love and self-honor within, etc.)?

For some additional inspiration, here are a handful of *my* real affirmations, which I wrote down daily as I was building my career as a singer, performer, actress, and all-around artist:

- ★ I am singing my heart out in the studio with ease and grace.
- ★ I am singing on stage joyously like a musical ministry, bringing joy and encouragement to others.
- ★ I am blessing the soul of people through my works.
- ★ I am happily watching myself act in projects I feel great about.
- ★ I am experiencing joy and touching the hearts of people around the world with my music.
- ★ I am excitedly touring and making great money.
- ★ I am giving thanks that my music is being licensed, and I am performing the music in various productive and positive outlets.
- ★ I am rejoicing that my music is being sold and played all over the world.

I have even created affirmations about my intentions with this very book you are holding right now!

- ★ I am reading my book with a smile on my face.
- ★ I am delighting that my book is being sold all over the world and is a top seller.

Now, go write down your own thoughts and turn them into brief and powerful sentence-long affirmations!

Mission, Purpose and Intention Exercise #3: Taking Stock of Your Life

If you still feel out of touch with your mission, purpose and intentions, I invite you to try one of the most successful ways I have found with what is most important and letting go of life's trivial matters.

When you are or one of your loved ones is sick and dying, all the non-sense disappears and what matters most comes forward. As morbid as it may sound, take a moment and imagine if this was your last day on earth.

- ★ *Now, ask yourself, "Have I done everything I want to do?*

Reflect on your life, your accomplishments, what is most important to you and what you are currently doing, imagining that today is your last day. Did you fulfill your dreams and live your life's purpose?

If your answer to this question is "no" ...

- ★ *Make a list of things you would feel you still need to do on this earth if you were living your last day.*

Really think about it! Do you have a "things I want to do before I die" list? Have you checked everything off it? Have you gone after everything you want every day, or are there still some things you want to pursue?

The beauty of checking in with yourself using this exercise is that it gives you the opportunity to rewind and list everything that is important to you so you can formulate intentions and go for them! Please do not wait until you are at that point to wonder what you could have done "if." Follow your dream and do what you want to do NOW!

Accountability Charts

Throughout this book, I will be providing you with charts to help you keep yourself accountable for the work you are doing towards strengthening your mind-body-spirit-emotions-environment connection. These accountability charts will help you get into a routine of self-care that will help you stay on task with manifesting your dreams and fulfilling your life's purpose.

Nurturing Your Mission, Purpose and Intentions: Accountability Chart

Use this chart to track your progress with defining and developing your mission, purpose and intentions each month. Every day you focus on the intentions you name on the left-hand side of the chart, give yourself a check mark!

ACCOUNTABILITY CHART

My intention is...

Example: To create beautiful paintings that bring joy to others' lives

	M	T	W	Th	F	S	Su	M	T	W	Th	F	S	Su	M	T	W	Th	F	S	Su	M	T	W	Th	F	S	Su

CHAPTER 2

Unleash Your Amazing MIND

"I will not let anyone walk through my mind with their dirty feet."
– Mahatma Ghandi

So as you think, so as you are, so as you will be. If you think negatively, it is easy to manifest negative energy around you. If you think positively, it is easy to manifest positive energy around you.

To put it another way: Whether you think you can do something, or you think you cannot do something, you are 100% right! Your actions are either supported by how you think, or suspended and paralyzed by how you think.

Seems pretty simple ... doesn't it?

Are you up for a little experiment? Great! Take a moment and think about a goal that you have for your life. It doesn't matter if this is a short-term goal or a long-term goal. Now, I want you to practice two ways of thinking about this goal. First, think to yourself "Oh, I can never do that. That's too hard. It will never happen." How does that thought make you feel? That doesn't feel too hot, does it?

Now, let's do the opposite. Think about that same goal, think of all of your talents, of all the things that you can offer the world, all the things that make you unique, all your gifts, and now think and speak it out loud "YES, I CAN DO IT." Say it loud; say it louder! (You may recognize this: It's one of those affirmations I just talked about!) Feel the power of what your mind can do when you think of things in a positive light – those thoughts alone generate energy, a will, a joy, a knowing that all things are possible.

The mind is the part of you that enables you to think. It is where your ideas, opinions, judgments, and thoughts swirl. Your mind is very powerful and more than capable of convincing you that you *can't* and you *won't*. It can activate you to take immediate action and to go full throttle ... or to completely shut down and give into the fear that will crush your strong, dynamic, brave and vibrant mind, body, spirit, emotions and even the environment in which you dwell.

Fear is a dream crusher!
We often pull back when we are afraid, even when we are going after something we really want. We are so afraid of being hurt or judged that we stop before our prayers are answered and before we achieve our dreams. You must be bold and set aside the fear and take the action steps to live what is in your heart.

I want to be very clear: We will all continue to feel fear when we encounter challenges in our lives. Therefore, seeking out a formula that completely eliminates fear is not the best use of your energy. (And just between you and me, you should be skeptical whenever anyone hands you a cut-and-dried formula for *anything*!) However, we can certainly find ways to bring forth the courage to do things in our lives that are heartfelt and to get through challenges in order to live out our ultimate purpose. We can develop strategies that get us past the fear of failure and towards manifesting our dreams. I believe we can let go of fear, connect with the love of what is most important to each of us ... and trust ourselves to move forward.

I often explore and talk about energy and how it flows through the universe, and that concept relates to fear as well. Because, energy can be positive ...or it can be negative, which is why we need to be careful of how we think. We can create what is on our minds, good or bad. So, why wallow in things that are negative or fear a horrible outcome when you can instead fantasize about life's amazing possibilities? It's very easy to get caught up in the fear of something we attempt not going well. But this practice ultimately paralyzes us from great accomplishment, which leads us to feel depressed about our lives. And what fun is that?

So, acknowledge that living what is in your heart can be a little scary sometimes, but then, just step through that pesky fear and go for it! What do you have to lose? Maybe you just let the last few weeks or months slip by ... or maybe you have been letting fear control you for years. Are you really willing to let another second go by without doing what you said you wanted to do? Let your thoughts drift away from fear, and towards being the best you possible!

How I Pushed through the Fear and Transformed My MIND
I remember back when I would just fantasize about making my *Spirit of Oya* CD. I dreamed about it for three years, but just never made it happen. I was writing songs, singing my little heart out, and I even had people at gigs asking me if I had an album for sale. I had some valid reasons why I could not go after it during that time, but some of them were just excuses. The truth is, when you really want to do something, you will do it. Tell me, what are *your* excuses for not going after your dreams?

Honestly, until I truly decided that I was going to get this album done, committed to the process and took the action steps necessary to bring it to fruition, that album was just not going to happen. On my birthday in January, I decided, with the help of my dear friend Marta and my now co-producer Ryan Cross – with whom I often perform – that this was the year! As I was blowing out my candle at a simple birthday dinner, I made a wish: I would complete my CD that year. I made a commitment to myself and to Ryan and told Marta to hold me accountable as a witness. I could not let myself down, nor could I let down those two lovely people who had been and would continue to be so supportive. I felt the need to finally create my own album in my soul, my gut and in my bones; the need was so deep that I had to honor it.

As I mentioned before, even after I declared I was going to do it, putting everything into action wasn't necessarily easy. I committed, but there were still many challenges that came up. There was other work, things happening in my life, the budget and how many thousands of dollars it was going to take to produce. And I was also working on my website (and that was a project in and of itself!). I wanted a certain type of studio that was going to allow for us to record all together at one time. And I wanted to work with the best musicians and to create the best project ever without spending hundreds of thousands of dollars. Then, of course, I had a lot of songs and had to narrow down the list to my favorites then write, re-write, edit ... the list of things I had to consider went on and on and was really overwhelming.

My mind said, "Oh my gosh ... what have I committed to? How am I ever going to get this done?"

With so many concerns weighing on me, I decided to take two days off, go away and get a hotel with peaceful scenery, away from the office work, paperwork and productions that I would get wrapped up in on a daily basis. I escaped from the constantly-ringing office phone, from talking to the next corporate gig advisor, director on a show I was working on and any brides or grooms hiring me for their wedding. I focused on my mind, planned my attack, and ... eventually, everything started to flow towards me!

Once I took the project seriously, the project started taking me seriously. Doors started opening. Amazing musicians that I could only dream up were suddenly interested and available on the exact dates that I chose, and my dream studio appeared, which would allow for all of us to perform at one time. Mysteriously, a song that I had not even considered appeared on my laptop. The hook was on my computer, but there were no lyrics. It turned into "Voodoo," which is now considered by many who have heard it to be one of the strongest songs on the album. And funnily enough, it discusses the fear, the negative thoughts and things we can do to ourselves that prevent us from manifesting what we say we want in our lives. The lyrics encourage us to stop blaming others for holding us back and to take a stand and take responsibility if we want to rise. And this song with a beautiful message was created while I was putting all my energy into nurturing this project.

In the end, the year I committed to putting out my CD turned out to be one of my best years of my life! And that happy post-CD-release train just keeps chugging along! I put out my first music video for my original song "Love," and more followed, including a video for my cover of "Accentuate the Positive," which I solely produced and directed. Now I am selling the album worldwide, and I am delighting in each additional music video I make and performance I give to support *Spirit of Oya*. The fabulous moment when this project finally came together and all these additional accomplishments would have never happened if I had not pushed through my fear.

The moral of the story is, we can always find a reason not to let our beautiful rays of light shine. But we all need to focus on all the reasons to let them shine bright for the whole world to see. If there is something aching in your heart, shouting out to be manifested, why do you continue to reject it month after month and year after year?

You can either let your mind be fueled by fear, or let it be fueled by spirit. If you choose to let your mind be fueled by spirit, you must change the way you think ... right now! The thoughts in your mind support your unflinching spirit, and all other elements of the 5 Star Points system. Skeptical? Think about it! The thoughts you have in your mind affect how you feel about your physical BODY and what you do with it ... just as they affect how full or empty your SPIRIT feels. And you decide the EMOTIONS you feel in every situation based on the thoughts you are having ... and make decisions about how the spaces around you influence your life, attitude, and ability to create based on the thoughts they spark. Since all 5 Star Points within you are working together, if one is unhealthy, the whole system breaks down.

With that in mind, would you rather let fear overtake and envelop you like a chaotic tsunami ... or let your strong and capable MIND, BODY, SPIRIT, EMOTIONS, AND ENVIRONMENT lift you up above the fear and help you fly?

Be the Boss of Your Thoughts

Even though the spirit is the driving force that gets us going, I often say that everything starts with the mind, because I fully believe we can create our reality. Do you believe that? If you do not, consider this: What you choose to see, hear, and engage in creates your reality.

So many people live life believing they are holding themselves accountable for the thoughts they have, yet have no idea why they are stuck. They are living in poverty with an equally impoverished mentality. They are repeating, "I'm broke," "I can't catch a break," "I will never make it through." The issue is, these people are stuck in the mire of the low-down vibrations they are creating by repeating refrains of hopelessness. Whether they know it or not, they are creating a negative outcome by perpetuating despair, attracting more and more of what is dragging them down.

If the idea of being powerful enough to create your own reality does not resonate with you yet stay patient, and keep reading. As you get deeper into exploring and working the 5 Star Points system, and take charge of the thoughts within your mind, you will start to feel the positive vibes flowing alongside all that inner peace and joy that comes from pursuing your dreams. Your perspective and your brain chemistry will change as you become the boss of your thoughts!

How will your mind change? First of all, you will learn to respect your own process and the process of others. Your judgments about both what others do and yourself will fade and disappear as you focus on yourself and put out and take in great energy. Similarly, the negative energy will no longer have a hold of you, whether it is coming from the inside, from others, or from your environment. There is, of course, war going on, and horrible things in the world, but your mind will be trained to rise above the darkness and, as one of my favorite songs, written by the great Harold Mercer in 1944 (which I covered on my CD!) goes, "accentuate the positive!"

When you rise above the chaotic negativity, your mind will feel free to...

★ Find solutions rather than complain about unsolvable problems.

* ★ See how you can actively further your purpose and help others rather than being "all talk."
* ★ Start to take actions steps that contribute to your own success and the success of those nearest and dearest to you.
* ★ Release your fears so you can use your mind as a powerful tool to help you manifest everything you want in your life.
* ★ Welcome in the unique brilliance of your life force and allow it to radiate from every pore.
* ★ Stop daydreaming and wishing, and start doing!

Your mind will be open to create and reflect on how you think and feel, so you can create a new and beautiful reality and come into your own gifts and talents.

Feed your mind!

Because of the work I do, I often have the pleasure of coming into contact with many amazing and creative people who shine bright, reach high and stand out above the crowd with their positive vibrations. But I also meet others who are dimming their lights and giving into negative thoughts in order to "fit in" or "stay under the radar." Maybe your dream is not to be a performer or someone else who regularly stands center stage in the spotlight ... but don't you want to live each day knowing you are important, loved, and that what you think, do, and say matters? Don't you want to be celebrated for the unique gifts you bring to the table?

The power of our mind and our thoughts is truly miraculous. They live in our mind and create our life. For better or worse, what we think dictates our actions, reactions, and emotions. What we feed our mind, what we allow in to take root and grow, creates either healthy or unhealthy thoughts.

Have you ever thought about what you feed your mind? Yes, you heard me! Feed your mind! Just as we give our bodies nourishment, we also must provide the proper and healthy nourishment for our minds. So the question now is what are you feeding your mind? And who do you let feed your mind? Are you feeding your mind meals of negative thoughts, served to you by negative people ... or is your mind eating up positive, healthful thoughts that encourage you to pursue your dreams and live your life's purpose?

What you feed your mind influences how you think ... and how you think can totally transform your entire life. Everything you think and say has power, and you can and will start operating on a positive frequency when you have positive thoughts. You might feel that the negative thoughts you think and the chaotic pessimism that creeps into your mind have no repercussions, because no one else can hear or see them. But this could not be further from the truth!

A lot of us are constantly judging ourselves in our heads, going on and on about what we cannot do. We worry and obsess, and our inner dialogue prevents us from moving ahead. By feeding ourselves this steady diet of self-effacing thoughts, we are taking down our energy, depressing ourselves, and talking ourselves out of doing what we want to do with our lives.

No one is perfect. Most have been guilty of the following self-criticisms:

★ "This will never work!"
★ "I am not worthy."
★ "I am not good enough."
★ "Now is not the right time."

This constant chatter depletes our energy, and can absolutely keep us paralyzed.

Flip all those negative thoughts immediately! How we think about ourselves is exactly how we will experience everything in our lives.

★ "This is going to be fantastic!"
★ "I am a worthy individual; I deserve great things in my life!"
★ "I am more than good enough."
★ "Now is the time ... so let's do this!"

Change that channel!
The thoughts you tune in or out will determine your reality. Choose the nature of your thoughts as you would choose what to watch on

television. Do you want to be tuned into a channel full of destruction, darkness, and despair ... or tuned into one full of sunny hopefulness, positive action, and forward motion?

You have to start turning your life around by feeding your mind positive self-talk. Because, if you don't believe in yourself, who will? What can you do if your self-talk is typically negative? Well there's no other way to say it ... let's whip that mind into shape! And I don't mean "let's do it later" or "let's do it tomorrow" I mean "let's do it NOW!"

Rewrite Your Story

Sometimes our negative thoughts are not conscious, but they can still destroy the sanctity of the mind, and prevent it from doing its part to manifest your dreams. These hidden, low-vibration, rotten thoughts are based on subconscious systems and old, sad stories that took root in us years ago and never left.

I have some great news for those of us that have these leftover thoughts: We can rewrite the story! We can recondition our minds so that our conscious and subconscious can both operate from a loving, know-ing, self-respecting, positive, and self-honoring place. We can believe in ourselves again, and make the old stories a part of our past.

Excellence lives in all of us, and it is up to use to tap into it. We are all creators, and it is up to us to believe in ourselves and fully engage, to know who we are, what we stand for and what to believe. If you have had hard times in the past, or negative intergenerational family patterns like poverty, abuse, illness, or regret have hurt you, you must release them!

Replace thoughts about "I can't" and "I won't" with "I can and I will." Look at only the positive outcomes of your actions, and allow these positive outcomes to be reinforced. Does this seem impossible? Well, I know from first-hand experience that it can happen! I have arrived at a place where, underneath it all, I truly believe that no matter what obstacles are thrown in my path things will always work out for the high-est good of all concerned. The self-loving path may take longer some-times, but it is totally worth it!

I have had ups, and I have had downs. I have lived in a place of total chaos, and lived in a place of harmonious delight in every day. I have agonized, and I have let the past go. And you know what? It will always be just fine! It took me a while to get to this place, and I am still a work in progress, but I just do not worry the way I used to when I am put in a challenging situation. I no longer even see challenging situations as "problems." I just focus my mind on the resolution and trust it will work out – that the story will have a happy ending.

It feels a lot like magic sometimes, but I know every story ends happily for me because of all the work I have put into my thought process. My conscious mind focuses on the positive so quickly that my subconscious mind just does not have a chance! It must succumb and support all the optimistic vibrations that are surging through me.

If you are not sure you believe me, let me ask you … How is staying stuck in what "always" has been before, or in your past negative experiences and thoughts working for you? Are you exactly where you want to be? Do you feel empowered and strong every day, even in the face of drama and turmoil around you?

Here is what I believe with all my soul: We have nothing to lose by embracing a positive mindset. It feels good, safe, secure, and powerful to live in a high, hopeful vibration. Of course, living this way is definitely a decision. I just know that ever since I decided to live this way, my spirit is thriving, and I am really living again. I am at peace, and the stress I once had has melted away. I feel good physically, emotionally, and the environment inside and where I live is stable and full to the brim with joy. When I changed the way I thought about my ongoing story, all 5 Points started to line up, and the sailing was smooth!

Do me a favor: When you start feeling that negativity from your past creep in, kick it out! And don't be nice about it – kick hard! Take control of those thoughts … and then feed your mind delicious, juicy, positive morsels … think them, shout them, and scream from the rooftops, "I CAN DO IT!!!"

"Do … or Do Not. There is No Try." – **Yoda**

What does Yoda have to do with the 5 Star Points? Everything! This is one of my favorite quotes and it supports an important part of changing your mindset and living out the philosophy of the 5 Star Points system with authenticity and enthusiasm.

Just listen to how this sounds: "I am going to try and ..."

Does that sound like the beginning of a powerful, fierce, no-nonsense statement about a definitive action? Does that sound like the battle cry of a capable, talented person who is going places?

Of course not! Many of us were told, "It's the effort that counts," or "A for effort" when we failed to accomplish a goal. While effort is certainly important, tackling a goal with the thought in your mind that just trying is enough is not going to make all your dreams come true. While you certainly need to cut yourself a break sometimes and even adjust your timeline for achieving an important goal when life takes you by surprise, I encourage you not to let yourself off the hook so easily!

Why? I, for one, do not want my mind to get in the habit of thinking I am just "trying." What is the purpose of trying? If you set out to do something special that will completely change your life with the idea that you will just "give it your best shot," I can guarantee you that it is not going to happen. If you are wishy-washy about your resolve to complete a project, you will never put your whole heart into it.

For example, what if I said, "I am going to try and put out a CD on September 23"? By saying "try," I have already pulled back from my intention of getting the CD out by that date. I am actually telling my brain it is OK to quit and fail to follow through. I am not holding myself fully accountable for my thoughts or for successfully achieving my important goal of getting that CD out.

Instead, I need to say, "I am happily releasing my CD on [DATE]!" I can see it, feel it, taste it, smell it ... I have declared it without a doubt, and it *will* happen.

We often do not see the critical connection between what we say and what we do – do not hold ourselves accountable for turning our thoughts into real-world actions. There is a war going on in our own mind between wishy-washy thoughts, and the mighty dreams we want to manifest with all our might. And this battle can make us wonder why the things we truly desire are not materializing out of thin air.

Do Your "I Am"s!

Instead of "I will try to," how about "I am"? It is amazing how two little words can have such a wonderful effect on the mind: I AM. They are two of the most powerful words in the world; what you say or write after them can build your entire reality.

"I am" comes from the ancient Hebrew name for God, and what you add to this phrase can empower you or disempower you right quick! As we discussed at the beginning of this chapter, so as you think, so as you say, so shall you be, and you must take particular care when saying "I am," because it means business!

If you use "I am" in a negative way, it can knock you down flat:

- ★ "I am scared."
- ★ "I am confused."
- ★ "I am sick."
- ★ "I am insecure."
- ★ "I am poor."
- ★ "I am ugly."
- ★ "I am stuck."

However, when used to further your mission and purpose, "I am" can free your mind and allow you to be who you are at your heart's core, and this is why you want to conjure it on a daily basis. It is the key to giving real oomph to your intentions and to reprogramming your mind. When you use "I am" for the greater good, what was once closed can be opened, and your light will shine!

- ★ "I am confident."
- ★ "I am enlightened."
- ★ "I am healthy."
- ★ "I am secure."

- ★ "I am rich."
- ★ "I am beautiful."
- ★ "I am free."

You need to be aware of the language you are using with "I am." "I am" is who you are: your real, authentic self. It is what you represent, and the center of you. It is a great reminder, healer, and motivator when you forget why you were put on this earth. When you make it a part of your daily life, magic will happen.

If you have disconnected from your core, or abandoned your authentic self and are working towards getting back in touch, these pure "I am" words will lead you there. They will help you proclaim who you are, what you represent, and the power of everything that is within you. "I am" affirms the truth of who you are and the limitless possibilities of what you will become.

I have been doing my "I am"s for years, and I now delight looking back on some of the older ones and seeing how many of them have come true or are in the process of coming true. Some of them, like this book, took a little while, but I am focusing on the positive fact that it is here now, just as I did with my CD. My "I am"s chronicle my success story, and allow me to see my own evolution as an artist, speaker, author and entrepreneur. These "I am"s through the years let me see the connections between my beginnings as a young lady starting my first successful business in high school, to the savvy business woman and artist I am today.

Even if you do not feel the "I am" today, you will if you continue to use it in your daily life. These words have physical power, and this awareness can change your life!

Break up with Your Resistance!
Sometimes we are resistant to moving forward with the pursuit of our dreams, especially when these dreams are particularly near and dear. And if your mind is unwilling to break up with this resistance, you are probably in for a struggle.

Why are you resistant?

When you think about it, resisting finally pursuing your dream sounds a little silly. It seems like the opposite of how our minds would react to such an opportunity. If this is really your heartfelt dream and life purpose, why would you not run to the finish line with no breaks, no discussions, and no nonsense?

I know the answer! When we are faced with finally grabbing a hold of something dear to us, our hearts will pull back. The very thing we love the most will cause us to recoil. We get angry with our friends or ourselves when all we or they do is talk about the dream without doing anything to chase it. Opportunity after opportunity lands in our laps, and we do nothing about it.

We pull back because we are simply afraid. (There's that fear monster again!) When faced with something so precious, we are afraid to move forward, because the worrisome thoughts overtake us: What if it does not work, and we are left with nothing? What if we go for it and find out we or it is not good enough? You might also be afraid you will be judged, ridiculed, or made fun of ... or you might be afraid of failure, believing that if you fail, you will have nothing left to live for.

And so, we refuse to break up with our resistance. We do not do it, because we are afraid, so we protect ourselves by doing nothing.

I am here to challenge you to find out what is blocking you and what is holding you back ... and to give resistance a voice, so you can shut it up right here and now!

Let me give you some examples of the deep, dark, ugly voice of resistance:

★ "I am resistant, because if I write this book, it could be terrible, and no one will care, and my big dream of being a huge author will disappear, and I will be nothing."

★ "I am resistant to move forward with my album, because if I go into the studio, the producers could say I am horrible, and my dream of being a rapper will be crushed."

- ★ "I am resistant, because if they turn down my script, that means I am not worthy of becoming a professional screenwriter."
- ★ "I am resistant, because if I go on auditions, and they do not choose me for the part, then that is telling me I am not a good actress, and I will have to get a regular job, and life will be over."

Even though your resistance is just your mind trying to protect you from what it perceives as potential disappointment and pain, you need to cut it out! Believe that you have the talent to thrive as a brilliant, creative being, push aside the resistance, and go for it!

Be honest with yourself: Do you have what it takes? I know you do, but you have to believe in yourself, or you are not going to be able to live your dream. Most of the people I have coached throughout my career just knew they had something, even those who struggled with the demons of self-doubt.

When you come up against rejection, disappointment, or the need to slightly alter your course, just remember, it is only temporary. What I am about to say may sound harsh, but *not everyone will like you*. This does not mean you are terrible at what you do or that you should throw in the towel. Not everyone likes the same style, the same type of voice, the same kind of writing, clothes or the same types of any other creative works. If you break up with your resistance, seek out the audience that will sing your praises, and keep working towards your mission, purpose, and intentions, there is just so much opportunity for you to shine!

I will admit that when I first started pursuing my dream to be an artist, singer, and entertainer, I was not 100 percent sure it was going to work. Some members of my family did not believe that making music was a viable career choice, so their nay-saying was crowding my own mind. I watched my peers in the music industry complaining about their finances and wondered how I could put myself through the same challenges.

Thankfully, I broke up with resistance. Soon, I started booking job after job, and found myself swimming in a lovely sea of positive reinforcement. I knew music was in my heart, and that I could sing. But it was not until I believed in my mind I could do it and stopped resisting that the proof was in the pudding. I, Oya Thomas, am making real money from individuals, corporations, promoters, and fans that allows me to do what I love. This is working, and I am earning what I need to take care of myself, reinvest in my company, and enjoy my life!

Are you ready to free your mind, and really go for it?
I cannot tell you how many times I have heard someone say, "I am a dancer," but then have no video or other proof of any dancing abilities ... how many times I have heard, "I am a songwriter," only to find out this person has not written down or recorded a single song. If you are what you say you are, you need to have the material to back it up, so you can proudly present your talents to others! Otherwise, how will anyone take you seriously enough to hire you? And how will you ever be ready to seize the opportunities that will help you realize your goals?

If you want to live your dream, you have to really go for it! Do not try for a week or two. Do it until it sticks! Go big or go home! No more griping about how hard you are trying to "make it" when you do not even have a plan and have not created any of the materials you need to pursue your creative mission. No more hemming and hawing, letting months pass you by without booking any gigs, shows, or jobs, only to say, "The industry sucks! I just can't catch a break!"

Whether you speak to yourself out loud or not, start thinking, "I am going to do this!" Be responsible, proactive and serious and do not allow fear to talk you out of realizing your dream. Get that head on straight, and forge ahead with confidence!

MIND Exercise #1: Organize Your Thoughts
★ *Practice organizing your thoughts by writing them down on paper as they come to you.*

When you are aware of your own thoughts and thought patterns, you can better understand your mind, purpose, and intentions. And organizing your thoughts helps you gracefully and easily manifest your dreams so you can live your life's purpose. Your thoughts can feel overwhelming when they are just bouncing around in your head, but when written down, they can feel manageable.

Meditate on a big dream that you want to come true then write down your thoughts as they come to you. Practice organizing them into categories! I think you'll be surprised!

MIND Exercise #2: Visualizing Your Mind's Reality

★ *Check in with your mind and where it is today ... then visualize where you would like it to be.*

Part of reprogramming your brain for positive, active thinking is understanding where it is today and the reality it is creating for you, so you can find your flow and move gracefully towards your goals.

What does your mind tell you when you think about going after your most heartfelt dream? If you are not sure what your most heartfelt dream is, ask yourself what you can see yourself doing that would be a true labor of love and would not feel like "work." Write all these thoughts down.

Now, try to visualize the actual steps you would need to take to turn this labor of love into your life's work. Write down any detail you can think of (and remember – no negative thoughts allowed). Visualize yourself manifesting your dream, and use your senses to feel, see, and experience what it would be like to cross the finish line!

MIND Exercise #3: Positive Self-Talk and "I Am" Affirmations

★ *Create your first set of "I am" affirmations to get into the habit of positive self-talk.*

Turn positive "I am" affirmations into an every-day habit in order to re-program your mind into believing in your intentions. Make a declaration of what you would like to see manifest itself in your life; use activating language that describes what you DO want vs. what you DO NOT want.

For instance,

★ "I am beautiful just the way I am."
★ "I am worthy of love."
★ "I am brilliant and capable of making my dream of becoming the best [insert creative discipline here] come true."

Write these "I am"s down and speak them aloud. Repeat them over and over again and breathe life into them. Give them legs! Then, give them wings! Release your mind, and be who you are at your heart's core. With practice, you will find yourself becoming comfortable with "I am," and starting to take the proper action steps to turn these words into your reality and let that light shine!

Nurturing Your Mind: Accountability Chart
Use this chart to track the progress you make strengthening your connection to your MIND each month. Put self-nurturing activities you engage in that feed your mind on the left-hand side, and every day you focus on the activities listed, give yourself a check mark!

ACCOUNTABILITY CHART

I am nuturing my mind this month by...

Example: Writing down "I am" affirmations to practice postive self-talk

	M	T	W	Th	F	S	Su	M	T	W	Th	F	S	Su	M	T	W	Th	F	S	Su	M	T	W	Th	F	S	Su

CHAPTER 3

Electrify Your Powerful BODY

Physical fitness is not only one of the most important keys to a healthy body, it is the basis of dynamic and creative intellectual activity. **– John F. Kennedy**

You cannot manifest your dreams and live your life's purpose if your body is physically unwell. Physical health is a means to taking action on your intentions and living your mission. Much as spiritually you cannot surround yourself with dark words, images and people and expect not to take some of that mindset on, you cannot eat a bunch of junk food and be lethargic and expect to be totally fit.

In order to illustrate the importance of your body to establishing an unshakable mind-body-spirit-emotions-environment connection and fulfilling your life's purpose, I want to tell you a story about how I learned to listen to mine.

I remember a time as a young woman when I was very concerned with my commitment to work out. And I confess, many times, I would neglect to take good care of my body. Working in the entertainment industry, which is notorious for the pressure it puts on both women and men to stay fit and look gorgeous at all times as a singer, actress, and performer, I wanted to work out for myself and my own peace of mind ... but also to look good for the camera.

Of course, as with anything else, one of the truths I did not embrace at the time is that the only way you can look and feel truly magnificent about your body is when you are keeping it healthy for yourself and not others. What do I mean by this? Rushing to lose weight for an audition or a job … or even your wedding in order to look good in front of others does not typically help you keep it off. Though a big audition, a major show, or your wedding are all important events, losing weight in order to fit into a dress and look good in that moment instead of to be healthy and like the image you see in the mirror every day is somewhat superficial. Really losing weight and making a commitment to be physically healthier is about a total lifestyle change, not a quick fix diet, or a way of eating and being that you cannot maintain.

My issue back in the day was not so much about working out, because I had that down; it was about eating – nourishing my body. While some try to fight overeating, my issue with food has always been about *not* eating. I would get so caught up in my work that I would overlook breakfast, snacks, water, lunch, and even dinner. And then, because I was not eating properly, I would barely have the strength to work out and keep my body in ship shape. And when I would travel, I would use the excuse that there was not great food available, so I would once again avoid eating altogether or give in and eat something that did not really give me the nutrients I needed to keep going.

Yes, there was a time when I was not eating right or taking care of myself. I believed I was fully focused on work, but in reality, I was just not feeling physically well enough for this to truly be the case. I was not getting proper sleep, then wondering, "Why am I getting sick all the time?" I had chronic sinus issues and miserable colds that seemed to stick to me like glue. And we all know that phlegm, coughing, and drainage does not work well with a singing career. It steals your vocal range and completely compromises your performance.

I was driving myself physically into the ground. As artists, we might get away with this for a while, but eventually, because our spirit dwells within us, we cannot create if the body is worn-down, tired, or sick.

Your Body, Your Sacred Temple
Aside from not eating, my other issue was stress, which took a very serious toll on my body. Thankfully, I learned fairly quickly that taking care of the temple that is your body is non-negotiable. My song "Too Blessed

to Be Stressed" references a time I visited a doctor who turned out to be exactly the doctor I needed at this physically unhealthy time in my life. Though she specialized in western medicine, she was very much into spirituality and how the mind and emotions can affect your body. There is almost always more than meets the eye when it comes to physical health issues and diseases of the body; physical symptoms often manifest when there is an issue within self that needs to be addressed and resolved. Many of us torment our bodies and feed it poison on a regular basis, work them to the bone without proper rest, still expecting those bodies to have the get-up-and-go needed to live our demanding lives.

When I was 19, I was super stressed out, going to college without much support. My parents did not know the first thing about college, and the production company I had launched at the same time was definitely not something they supported, not because they did not want me to pursue my dreams, but simply because they did not understand. I was at odds with my mom and barely speaking to her, because I felt she did not accept who I was and the choices I was making. And because she and I were constantly arguing, I was also unable to talk to my father, because she was the one who manned the phone in their home.

I was also having issues with my so-called boyfriend at the time. Like my parents, he was not supporting me and my dreams, and our relationship was unhealthy as a result. He hated the entertainment industry and wanted me to focus on college so I could be a "successful" corporate woman. My boyfriend would regularly belittle me and my "little production company" with each booking. He just did not get the picture. He did not appreciate the arts and thought that both my company and my hope I could turn it into something great and also be an artist myself were silly. He warned me and argued with me about how unstable my dreams were, and how no one really makes real money doing what I wanted to do. And because my parents did not understand anything about college or the entertainment industry I wanted to work in, they kept pushing me to get a state job with benefits – to be a "success" so they could be proud of me and tell their friends I had what they perceived to be a good, solid job. With all the chaos around me, I holed up in my apartment and stopped talking to everyone else. I tried to figure it all out for myself.

Maybe you can see where this story led. Maybe you have even been here before yourself! One day, I became very physically ill. I did not even know what was happening at first, because I had always been very healthy. To not feel good physically all over was just strange to me. It was not the flu or a cold. My back just did not feel right, and my body ached, and I could not explain it. I ignored it and went about my business, but a few days later, after an argument with my boyfriend, while struggling with my thoughts about what I wanted to do with my life alone in my apartment, the pain in my back intensified. I went to use the restroom, and noticed there was blood in my urine. I was in excruciating physical pain, and I called my brother, who took me to the emergency room.

The doctor determined I had a urinary tract infection that was turning into a bladder infection. I was told to start a course of antibiotics, get rest, and drink plenty of water. I thought, "That's it?" After a few pills, gallons of water and cranberry juice, and a few solid naps, I was back in business ... or was I?

While my body felt physically somewhat better, I was in reality just "back in the business" of combating more drama, day in and day out. Not surprisingly, I went back to my old way of being, and three months later, I had another urinary tract infection ... and then a few months later, another. Each time I would get antibiotics, and they would get rid of my physical symptoms, but the infection would come back. Even the doctor recognized this was not normal. She was concerned that I had a cyst or tumor of some sort, so she sent me to a specialist.

As I waited for the verdict at the doctor's office, paranoid and stressed, my mom sat in the waiting room, probably just as scared as I was. I realized that no matter what drama we were going through, she was there for me. She did not necessarily agree with or understand the life I was choosing for myself, but she was there. And I realized I just was not happy. I also realized I did not want to feel like this. And here I was, physically ill and vulnerable.

The doctor finally came in and told me that nothing was physically wrong with me. This should have been great news, but instead of feeling relieved, I felt frustrated: Why was my body not cooperating? Why was I not physically healthy? I expressed my frustrations to the doctor, and she said, "You do not have anything now, but you will get something if you do not learn to manage your stress. You will create a cyst or tumor. Whatever you are dealing with, you need to let it go. You need to get back to your happy self and live."

I was only 19, and negativity and stress already had me in its grips! And it was affecting my physical body. I cannot even remember this doctor's name today, but her words changed my life. She taught me that stress is a waste of energy that will make me sick. And at 19, I realized I had too much going on and that I did not want to end up in a hospital bed for anyone or anything. I had a life to live, and dreams to realize. I was and still am "too blessed to be stressed."

Today, my life can still be a challenge, but I do not let it get to me. The way I work through stress is now totally different. (And I have never once had a reoccurrence of a UTI, which shows me there was a direct correlation between experiencing high levels of stress getting sick.) When I feel overwhelmed with a million things to do, my problem is almost always time management, and the stress I feel is not negative. I am happy that I have so much to do with my life's purpose. I am doing what I enjoy, delegating when I can, and feeling the love.

Establish a schedule to protect your temple.

As an artist, sometimes staying on a strict schedule goes against our voice, but we have to establish a schedule that will allow us to rest, eat right, and exercise, no ifs, ands or buts! Our body is our temple, and our spirit is housed within this body. The physical body plays host to your spirit's good work, so you need to be rested and ready to get up, get down, get on the good foot, create, and live!

Sometimes staying on a schedule is a challenge, and I will admit that I do not stay on a perfect 8-hour sleep schedule, nor do I work out every single day. But I do the very best I can, and I do pretty well! I miss chunks of time sometimes, but I go a little easy on myself, then make my way back to the gym, take my walk, go to my yoga class, or get active ASAP so I am never too far away from it.

Keeping a Healthy Body is a Commitment to Yourself
Maintaining a strong and able body is a lifestyle change and a commitment. It is about being disciplined and practicing healthy habits every day. Of course, all the 5 Star Points are important and must be taken seriously and worked into your life every single day, so you can be the best you and have all your faculties intact. But you need to be feeling physically great so you can pull the very best out of your heart and soul.

I set myself up for success and energized living by making sure I always have nourishing food in the house, so that even when I am in the thick of creating, I can reach for a healthy snack. I have to remind myself that ordering in something healthy is OK sometimes, but it has to be a "sometimes" event vs. a regular habit. I have instructed my assistant to call me to task on this, so she can support the positive choices I want to make for my body.

The last video I produced, directed and was in, one of my assistant's main tasks was bringing me water, an apple, or a banana throughout the day to keep me nourished and hydrated. Even though I believe I have learned my lesson about not neglecting my health, sometimes I can still get so busy that I forget to take care of my physical body.

If you are in the same boat, make tending to your temple a regular habit! Keep a jug of water in front of you, pack your snacks, set alarms to remind you if you must, or have an assistant or friend remind you to replenish your fuel on a schedule. You may be thinking going to this extent to fulfill a basic need is silly: "I am not a child! I can take care of myself!" But the fact that it is a basic, fundamental need is exactly why tending to it is so imperative. If your body is not feeling powerful and in top form, you will not be able to manifest those beautiful dreams of yours and empower yourself to reach for the greatest heights!

Honor Your Body
Physically, I am feeling the best I have ever felt in my life. I am eating right, exercising, sleeping and making time for massages to put

my body in the calm and peaceful place that allows me to create. In fact, right now, I am sitting here writing this book with a nice, tall glass of water with fruit in it, having just eaten a well-balanced meal. I feel good right down to the tips of my typing fingers! As you are reading my words, you can feel confident that you are getting my best. I am in a solid state of mind and spirit because I have been taking good care of myself. And as a result, my emotions and environment are also supporting me every step of the way.

I implore you: Honor your body and keep it happy and healthy. Your spirit and mind are counting on your body to think happy thoughts and be healthy so you can realize all your dreams and fulfill your life's purpose!

Your body deserves respect!

My father used to tell me, "It's so easy to get in trouble, but hell to get out of it."

Boy oh boy was he right! I have taken this statement with me my whole life. We have to be very careful what we get into!

Have you said any of the following statements before?

- ★ "I will do anything to be a star."
- ★ "I will do anything to make my product launch."
- ★ "I will do anything to _____."

Will you really? At what price? Are you willing to compromise everything you believe in? Are you really willing to sell out?

In the entertainment industry especially, but in any workplace, we can easily get caught up in thoughts of, "If I just do this one thing, I can get that raise or promotion." And there are sometimes dark people around who will try to get us to compromise our values and ourselves with promises of money, prestige, stability or "success" in exchange for sex, illegal activities or other actions that go against our soul and spirit.

Are you really willing to give away your body and temple and compromise your character and integrity for a "quick fix" or to get on the fast track?

It took me three years to get out my CD, because I personally financed it, hand-picked the best of the best musicians, producers and other partners and did it on my own terms. Even though the process was not always easy, I know I own my project, and I did not rip my whole soul or engage in behaviors that were not self-loving just to make my dream happen. As big of a deal as making an album was to me, I knew it was not worth selling my soul or offering up my body to the highest bidder.

No one wants to talk about that dark energy that enters with promises of "helping" you achieve your dreams, but is really out to put you on a detour from your mission. It can really hurt you. You know giving into this energy is not a good idea, but you want to get to the finish line and realize your dreams so badly that you feel you are willing to do anything. I'm not necessarily just talking about having sex with someone you do not want to – sleeping your way to the top, though this has been going on since the beginning of time and across many industries, for both men and women.

My point is not to judge, but if you are selling yourself in exchange for something you want, turning yourself into a product that can be bought and sold, you have turned yourself into a slave. Yikes! I know that sounds harsh, but it is the truth. And your body and soul are much too valuable for that nonsense! When you become a "product" with a price tag, you degrade the delicate mental, physical, spiritual, emotional and environmental balance within and outside yourself.

A beautiful actress I know mentioned to me that a producer told her, "Too bad you are dating someone, because you would have a three-picture deal by now," implying that if her body were "up for grabs," she would be able to advance her career.

She wanted her career to take off so badly, and his words made her feel dirty, powerless and physically ill. They made her question her ability to stay strong in the industry and wonder whether engaging in these types of "fast track" activities was the only way anyone could have a career.

She has made it a point, much as I have, to surround herself with artists who respect their bodies and themselves and work with producers and directors that approach every project with total integrity. These beings do exist, even in this industry! And they will come to you if you honor your body and yourself.

Taking "big money" from people for gigs that are not in alignment with who you are is unhealthy. Doing any project that does not make you feel good just to get ahead can be a form of prostitution and can break you down, taking you far, far away from your mission and goal.

Your body is worth so much more than that! You can say yes to what you want and no to what you want. When you follow your own voice and honor your body, you will feel empowered.

The self-respecting, self-loving path may sometimes take longer, but trust me, it is so much more rewarding than the alternative! And at the end of the day, when you look in the mirror, you will feel radiant, inside and outside!

Accept Yourself as You Are

If you are like the rest of us, there are probably many things you would like to change about your physical appearance. But many of us can get so wrapped up in change from time to time that we try to force ourselves into doing things that really do not fit who we genuinely are. Therefore, I believe that connecting with your body sometimes means accepting yourself as you are RIGHT NOW.

Now, by "accepting yourself as you are," I'm not talking about being lazy or continuing to practice unhealthy behaviors. I am not saying that if you realize you don't like to exercise, you shouldn't go for a walk, or that if you don't like to eat healthy, you should have donuts for break-fast every morning, and fast food for lunch and dinner, throw up your hands and say, "This is just who I am."

"Accepting yourself as you are" means that you have to accept real traits that you have and not be so hard on yourself or force yourself to change simply because you fear that others will not accept you and you think you need to change for them. I definitely do not believe you should compromise yourself to make your friends or a new significant other happy. You might "fit in" with these people short term, but you will eventually feel yourself slipping away.

Sometimes we all find ourselves compelled to change in ways that are not necessarily good for our mind-body-spirit-emotions-environment connection. Therefore, you have to ask yourself an important question when you are considering any type of transformation:

"Are you changing for yourself ... or for someone else?"

Is this change something that will help you grow and improve your life? Will this change uplift you, raise your vibration and spark your evolution into something bigger and better?

You can begin thinking about your own transformation by looking honestly within yourself at your many great qualities and the qualities within you that you might like to work on. (Remember that earlier exercise about identifying your most positive qualities? You should do it again and again for each of your 5 Star Points!) Then realize your transformation is not necessarily about "change," rather "acceptance." Accept who you are and then fully stand in your own beauty and shine your light.

Do YOU feel pressure to fit in?

So many of us are so worried about fitting in and not being judged – whether for our appearance, our thoughts, or anything else – that we try to change ourselves when what we need to be doing is accepting ourselves and standing in our own authenticity. And that glorious authenticity, that beautiful acceptance is our true power.

How can acceptance of ourselves be powerful?

When we accept ourselves, we let go of the judgments that we once had and can truly allow ourselves to be OURSELVES. The authentic "you" is beautiful, just as it is. And wouldn't it feel good not to have to put up a front or try to be something other than you are? Knowing that you are worthy and fantastic, just the way you are, is everything.

Acceptance can be a challenge when there are things about you that you do not like, but before you pass judgment on yourself, ask, "Do I not like these things because they make me not fit in, or because I'm afraid of what others might think of me or how they might judge me?" Before you release an aspect of yourself, think about whether letting go of it will truly make you a better person and allow your spirit to evolve, and make you feel and look better than ever!

So, go forth and make your change for the betterment of you. Then, accept yourself in all your glory!

Celebrate Your Body
Do you ever take your body for granted? You do not have to be a model, actor, or someone on camera, on stage, or in the spotlight to take care of yourself. If you are a woman, your body goal may not be to fit into a "perfect" size 2-6. If you are a man, you may not be aiming for a 32-inch waist. Still, we all need to strive for a healthy body that makes us feel happy to be in our own skin.

Take care of yourself, take time for yourself, and treat yourself, so you can always celebrate being you, glorious you! Save up and make special time to treat your body to experiences that make it feel rejuvenated and ready to take on all your days. If I can do it, so can you!

I am on the computer a lot, and I also work out, so it is important that I take an hour out of my schedule at least once a month for a massage. It is something that I want and need with all the rigors I put my body through. It feels good and works through any muscle knots that might want to try in sneak in. I get on the table, and I let the tension melt away!

Maybe a massage just isn't your thing. No problem! You can choose to take some time for something else that helps you release the tension and get in a physically relaxed space. Get your hair or nails done, get a body scrubs or a facial ... whatever you need! Just make this treat a MUST HAVE at least once a month. It will feel good to reward yourself for all the hard work you do! Acknowledge your work, show yourself some appreciation, and celebrate that body of yours!

Celebrate YOU and Your Learning Process

Sometimes when I sit down to write something, whether for my blog or another one of my projects, I find myself in a space where I am writing about exactly what I need. And the experience becomes about sharing not what I know, but what I am learning.

For the past couple years – ever since I resolved to put out my *Spirit of Oya* CD, I have been regularly thinking about how much I have been running, running, RUNNING and pushing myself to live this beautiful life of mine that is in progress.

I appreciate that I have the physical, mental, spiritual and emotional energy to run so much, as it allows me to reach my goals, but there are times that every marathon runner reaches his/her goal and needs to really celebrate!

"What?" you might ask. "Celebrate? What is that?" If you reacted that way, that is a problem. But I understand: As creative people, we all get in the habit of putting out project after project and just moving onto the next thing without even taking a breath.

I regularly find myself in conversations with clients and friends about the concept of taking a break, a vacation, about slowing down and just stopping to smell the roses. I certainly admire those who have the drive to keep going ... but we have to be careful, because there is a fine line between having a tireless drive to accomplish things and running yourself ragged. I know so many people who are afraid to stop, because they feel that if they stop, the world as they know it will fall apart, or that someone else will take their place. These people come to believe that there is never time for a break, and that kind of drive can really take a toll on your body!

When your labors of love start to turn into chores, and you become tired, taking just a few days off to relax, recharge and celebrate the wonderful work you have done can be very beneficial. Sometimes you can be so in the thick of everything that you might get stuck on questions that arise during a project. And you have to step away, take a break and then come back to give yourself some space so the answers will become clear.

Other times, when you finish a project, taking a moment to pat yourself on the back and acknowledge your good work is simply good for the soul. Because, if we just keep working, what does it all mean? Why are we even working? What is the reward? We need to take time to feel, recharge our physical bodies, and really enjoy that moment of accomplishment.

Get it while it's hot!

I know sometimes we have to "get it while it's hot." I understand the "get it while it's hot" mentality very well, and I often subscribe to it. However, even as you adopt this mentality, you need to take some time for yourself each month, quarter or year.

Now, focusing on yourself in this way can get tricky when you do what you love. For example, I often ask myself, "Why would I want to step away from my musical and artistic labors of love? Why would I want to get off the stage?" Well, this feeling of loving what I do actually helps keep me energized in all those 5 Star Points areas while I am enjoying time off. I get to bask in a weekend of relaxation, look at delicious food coming out, the beautiful resort, or feel the healing hands of a masseuse knowing what I do for a living is paying for all of it. I don't ever want my "work," or my "labors of love" to be a chore, or an exhausting, depleting job. Every time I walk on the stage, it is my intention to be fully charged, to give my audience my very best self ... and how could I do this if I was tired or run down?

Say, "No" to exhaustion.

So, I think a big lesson I have learned is, do not exhaust yourself so much that you cannot do what you love doing. HERE is your place to do what you do. And we can all look at our schedules and find a little "me" time to keep us well and energized, so our work will shine bright. We all must take care of our bodies – our temples, which allow us to physically get out there and create beauty.

I want to ask you an important question: Do you ever feel mentally, physically, spiritually or emotionally drained and closed in within your environment? Whether you love your job, or you don't, sometimes a little getaway is what you need. And sometimes taking a "getaway" doesn't even mean going anywhere at all. A getaway can be as simple as staying home and relaxing with your phone ringer and your computer turned off. In our connected society, this might sound crazy, but you can do it! Or, you can take a spa day or a beautiful drive up the coast.

The main point I want to stress is, a little R&R of the soul is GOOD for you. Having a clear mind, a healthy body and an aligned spirit will give you a free, beautiful, emotional flow. And breathing in a beautiful environment will allow you to start running again with a refreshed mind and strong body.

With that being said, I want to joyfully give you permission to plan a getaway party for YOU. Because, YOU are worth it and YOU deserve it. Celebrate! You're doing it!

So, when the time is right, take a day, a long weekend, a week ... or even a month to celebrate living your dream!

Beware of Flying Objects!

As you are trying to stay on task with a health regiment that supports your powerful body, beware of distractions that will fly at you, taking you off your path towards an enlightening, heart-centered life rooted in a solid relationship with your mind, body, spirit, emotions, and environment. You may not even recognize them as distractions at first, as they will often disguise themselves as elements that will bring you happiness and strengthen your core mission.

I am telling you this from a place of very recent experience, which goes to show you that even those of us on the path of our dreams sometimes go astray, especially when a pretty flower beyond the path catches our attention, or we see a tree that looks like it needs climbing.

While I have been on task the last couple weeks, a few weeks ago, I got a little distracted. On the surface I felt I was getting so much done, but when I actually gauged my progress, it seemed I was not getting anything done at all. I had been wandering away from my schedule, entertaining other bright and shiny lights that were entering my space. I connected with a talented songwriter who is well respected, but he does not do my type of music. And then another artist wanted to start a band that I did not have time for … and another musician wanted to form a duo and perform at hotels. These were all fantastic opportunities, but I had to ask myself, is any of this contributing to my mission, purpose and intention? Do I actually want this?

And you can bet my body told me exactly what was up. "You are in conflict," it said. My skin started to break out. I was not sleeping hardly at all or working out, and I just felt physically "off." These physical symptoms put me on high alert; I knew I had to let go of some of these distractions that were steering me off course. I had to get back to resting properly and getting back to my regular schedule. And you know what happened? As soon as I committed to getting back on track with my dreams, my skin, my sanity, and my spirit all returned to normal.

Love Your Body, Love Your Life!

There is so much for all of us to do in this life, but you must enjoy the time you have, and allow your body to be healthy, so your spirit can do its important work. Take heed and keep the positivity flowing: You are the physical manifestation of love, and if you are love, you can never be unworthy. Love yourself and love your body so it can work for you! People may say or do things that hurt us, but if you are approaching life from a loving place, nothing can touch you!

Manifest the physical appearance you want.

Remember what we talked about with the mind? What your mind focuses on is exactly what you will get. How do you want to look on the outside, and how can you make that physical appearance reflect your glowing insides?

First and foremost, you need to honor your temple in order to look and feel physically fantastic. Take the time to express yourself through your wardrobe, and fix your hair or makeup. Take pride and honor in keeping yourself fresh, with clean clothes that make you feel good about yourself on the inside and provide a window into your special soul. You do not have to wear designer clothes, but you do need to take pride in your appearance and let it express who you are and what you represent, so every time you step out, others know, without a doubt that you respect yourself, and therefore, they need to as well! Love yourself from the inside, out by taking the time to look absolutely amazing!

Create Your Own Healthy Body Routine

Do you have a regular routine for keeping your body – your temple – healthy, happy, and fully invigorated? If not, you need to make it a habit immediately! If you are regularly paying attention to your body, if you have any physical issues, you can nip them in the bud before they get out of control.

Show yourself and others that you honor and care about your physical health with the following sample BODY checklist:

- ★ **Diet.** A meal plan that includes healthy meals with snacks throughout the day and plenty of water. Avoid toxins, sugars, and too much salt.
- ★ **Rest.** A good, solid six, to eight hours of real sleep with no television on in the background and naps when you are working hard and need to give your body a break.
- ★ **Exercise.** The gym, walks, yoga, pilates or any other fun exercise plan to get your body moving and your energy swirling.
- ★ **Self-nurturing.** Massages, facials, haircuts and hairstyling, manicures and pedicures that give your body a "treat" and reward you for all your hard work.

Body Exercise #1: Body "I am" Affirmations

What are you telling yourself about your body? Do you believe it is a temple and a powerful machine that can help you triumph every day? How do you see yourself when you look in the mirror?

⭐ *Make a list of positive "I am" affirmations about your body.*

Write down some positive statements about your body using "I am" phrases that celebrate its best qualities and the powerful ways it helps you navigate your life. What do you like? What makes your body and the way you take care of, celebrate and honor it unique?

Here are some examples:

- ⭐ "I am a strong, resilient being with powerful legs capable of running ___ miles every day to stay fit and to raise my vibrations."
- ⭐ "I am having fun while losing weight and toning my body exercising, playing sports and dancing."
- ⭐ "I am a beautiful creature celebrating my life and expressing my inner joy by wearing clothing that I look fabulous in."
- ⭐ "I am fantastic at dressing myself, and I have a real talent for finding clothes that accentuate the best parts of my body."
- ⭐ "I am standing up straight tall and proud shining my light brightly."

Body Exercise #2: Devising a Diet, Exercise and Rest Plan

Establishing a routine for diet and exercise can help strengthen your body and prepare it to take on the hard work needed to reach your goals and have the energy to thrive during all of life's little challenges and triumphs!

⭐ *Put together a daily diet, exercise and rest plan that gives your body what it needs to flourish.*

Here are some tips for setting your own personal routine:

Think about your health and fitness goals. How do you want to feel every day? What do you like about your body and lifestyle, and what would you like to change about both?

Create a schedule that will allow you to ease into it. Start out thinking about small changes you can make to your current diet, exercise and rest plan (or lack of plan!) that will make commitment a no-brainer and keep your mind thinking positive thoughts!

Ease up on yourself when you go astray! Even I get a little out of sync with my routine from time to time. You just have to dust yourself off, and get back to it!

Body Exercise #3: Making a Date to Relax with Yourself
We all have to make time for pampering to practice self-love and give our bodies a little treat.

> ★ *Book a massage, facial, haircut, hairstyling session, manicure, pedicure, or whatever else you enjoy doing to make your body feel special.*

I mean it! Book it today! You will thank me for it later! And while you're at it, make it a regular part of your body care routine. Whether it's once a month, or once a week, treat your body like the special temple it is on the regular, and feel an almost instant boost in your mind-body-spirit-emotions-environment connection.

Nurturing Your Body: Accountability Chart
Use this chart to track the progress you make strengthening your connection to your BODY each month. Put self-nurturing activities you engage in that support your body on the left-hand side, and every day you focus on the activities listed, give yourself a check mark!

ACCOUNTABILITY CHART

I am nuturing my body this month by...

Example: Working out at the gym for 'x' hour(s)

	M	T	W	Th	F	S	Su	M	T	W	Th	F	S	Su	M	T	W	Th	F	S	Su	M	T	W	Th	F	S	Su

CHAPTER 4

Your Indomitable SPIRIT

"There is a light in this world, a healing spirit more powerful than any darkness we may encounter. We sometimes lose sight of this force when there is suffering, too much pain. Then suddenly, the spirit will emerge through the lives of ordinary people who hear a call and answer in extraordinary ways." **– Mother Teresa**

Your spirit is the non-physical core of you. Whereas your soul is your actual life, your spirit is your life force! Spirit comes from the Latin word "spiritus," which means "breath." It is also used to describe a person's consciousness – who they are when they are awake and what they experience.

My favorite thing in the world, and why I love the work I do is FEELING. Feeling is what it is to be alive and connected, and this is at the root of the spirit. The spirit is what it means to be alive and connected – not to merely have life and be a disconnected zombie, but to make the most of the gift of life, filled with joy and the spirit of you inside the vessel of the human form. You are a divine being having a human experience, living out your life's purpose, your dream and what you are here to do.

When people say, "You can kill me, but you can't kill my spirit," they mean that while the human soul can perish, the spirit lives on. Think of it this way: The spirit of musicians and songwriters who have passed away lives on through their music. Their physical bodies are no longer here, but their personality and their consciousness lives on through their works.

My dear, late father was named after the prophet Ezekiel from the book of Ezekiel in the Bible, and I often meditate on one of my favorite passages to remind myself of the deep connection between soul and spirit, from Ezekiel 18:4: "Behold, all souls are one; as the soul of the father, so also the soul of the son is mine: the soul that sinneth, it shall die."

Regardless of your religion or sense of spirituality, it is truly your spirit that gives you life and makes you the unique, capable, important human being you are. That being said, how do you define a life … how do you define your life?

Life and Force

Before we get deeper into the spirit piece of the 5 Star Points, let's take a closer look at the important and powerful concept of "life force" by breaking down its two components.

- ★ **life** *noun*
    - : to be in existence
    - : the mere existence of a human being or animal
    - : a period between birth and death

- ★ **force** *noun*
    - : the strength or energy as an attribute of a physical action
    - : power

As we think about beautiful life that keeps us all here on the planet and someone using force to get something done, we can see how the concept of "life force" and your spirit are inextricably linked.

Connect with Your Spirit

In a busy world where so many people are telling us what to look like, how to feel and how to live our lives, it can be challenging to take the time to genuinely connect with our spirit. Yet, even with all our busyness, we need to take the time to honor spirit. "Co-creating" with our own spirit from a heart-centered, driven place and with God is a huge part of connecting to your authentic self.

The idea that we each have a spirit inside us is so foreign to many, because we tend to get wrapped up in what is going on in the external world and what everyone around us is doing. I have learned from personal experience that it's so easy to get distracted and end up being far removed from co-creating and connecting with our heart. If we're not careful and let ourselves be distracted for too long, we will find ourselves far removed from our true mission and purpose.

You are a divine being, capable of sharing loving energy with the world, and we are all divine beings, sharing a real, human experience. This is why we should stop and take the time to check in with our spirit regularly: "What is my soul attempting to learn while I'm on this planet?"

It all starts with the mind-spirit connection!
I often say that improving your mind-body-spirit-emotions-environment connection begins deep in the mind and spirit. Adopting an attitude that has us quickly getting upset about everything that does not go our way and blaming others for all that is not quite right in our lives will not help enlighten our individual journeys and set us on a blessed path. If we approach every experience in life thinking, "What can I learn from this?" we will receive the special gifts that lead to profound growth.

Working on yourself and striving to become a more compassionate and loving person is the best way to find happiness, so I encourage you to set aside time to have meaningful conversations with your inner voice, and keep those dark thoughts out of your mind. After all, your life does not belong to anyone else but you; it is your gift and your chance to share, create and express yourself. The more you clear up unresolved issues within yourself, the less you accuse others of causing you to struggle and the less you project negative vibes onto others, the more deeply you connect to your spirit; your true gifts reveal themselves, and people see you change and begin to feel inspired to change themselves.

When you begin to heal and you shine your light, people experience your joy and see you as a source of loving change, encouragement and hope. Although you are just one person on the planet, when you adjust your mindset, your shift will prompt other shifts around you. So, as each individual finds peace, it causes a chain reaction that brings about a series of quantum shifts capable of healing others around the world.

Get in on the action!
In order to check in with where your spirit is at this very moment, look at your own actions — how you interact with the world. So many of us live, but do not think about our actions, or how they affect others and our universe:

- ★ Are your actions rooted in love, or in negativity?
- ★ How do you treat yourself ... and others?
- ★ Are your actions reflective of who you are at your core ... or are they being shaped by who the world expects you to be?

Sit back and really observe yourself ... and be honest! Examining how you treat yourself and others and making yourself accountable for your actions will reveal deep truths about your spirit. If you don't like what you observe — if your actions aren't the actions of the loving spirit you know is within you ... why aren't they? What has compelled you to act in a way that is out of character for the truth of YOU?

No more "should've-would've-could've"s!
The fact is, in order to make peace with your loving spirit, you must be truthful and behave the way your Spirit would want you to behave. And in order for all of us to accomplish this serenity, we must be careful about believing we know best — that we know how everything "should" be at all times. At some point, we've all found ourselves saying, "He should do this," or "She should have done this," or "I should have done something different." (Remember those "I am"s at all times!)

"Should" can be self-damaging, because it implies obligation, and it can lead to us judging ourselves and others. We need to respect that each of us has our own individual process. You can certainly look back on an experience and say, "I should have done it this way." I would encourage you to acknowledge what you learned from that experience, because, growth is a beautiful part of being human. And when you really learn a lesson from an experience that may seem like a "mistake" in hindsight, you will not have to repeat that struggle in the future. And that's great news! We all have different approaches, different lessons to learn and different lives to live. We need to respect our own process and the processes of others.

How far away are you from your spirit ... RIGHT NOW?

Once you've soaked in what I've written above, ask yourself, "Am I far removed from my spirit?" If your answer is, "Yes," it's okay. Don't get depressed about it! You are not alone. There are so many people that get caught up with life, work and just living that connecting with their Spirit isn't even on their radar.

Just be patient. You can slowly and comfortably start to take time to align with yourself by meditating on your heart and true thoughts, away from the craziness of day-to-day life. While getting away for a day or two is ideal, sometimes just taking a brief pause, a deep breath for a moment during your day can make a huge difference.

I personally love going away by myself for a day or two to regain a sense of clarity. And when I journal or just sit, think and connect, away from distractions like the ringing phone and emails, I get a sense of calm thinking about what is going on with me in the present and which dreams I am ready to manifest. I love getting calls and talking to clients, but we all have to quiet our minds, hearts and the external world and reach deep within to connect to our spirit so we can be centered as we move through our lives.

When you really connect with your spirit, you leave little to no room for negative self-talk, disbelief and doubt to sneak in. The connection and alignment between you and your core bring for wisdom and awareness of life and consciousness that opens up the possibilities for how you can think and create. You are able to use the power of your mind and spirit in a way that will change your life, and your creativity goes through the roof!

The awareness of your spirit affects everything: how you think; how you connect with your body; how you interact, respond and react to your emotions and how you are in your environment. When you connect to this space within you, you will connect with your love of self so much and be so determined in your soul that you will be able to do anything you set out to do.

Part of *my* purpose is to help others shine their light and connect with the love and wisdom they already have inside by using my 5 Star Points system. And it is my wish that those I help will spread the love and pass on these skills to others, until we have a world full of creative, hopeful beings, manifesting their heartfelt dreams and pursuing their true purpose.

You have spirit, yes you do!

When people are excited about someone's progress and accomplishments, even when that person is still stuck in a dark place, they often say, "He/she really has the spirit!"

But it goes even deeper than that: I believe connecting with your spirit means connecting with your life force – connecting with your reason to live. And that reminds me of mission, purpose and intentions. You may not be with me quite yet on this (however, I *know* you will get here!), but life is wonderful, and I give thanks for it every day, and that is why I choose to make every day a day I am following my dreams and living my life's true purpose. And, while it is true we all have "life" according to the basic dictionary definition, not everyone is really LIVING!

And I can assure you, because I have experienced it, that when you connect to your spirit, life and purpose, there is nothing that can replace that amazing feeling. When you are clear about your mission and purpose, no matter what happens in your life, you will know who you are and what you stand for, which is powerful and enables you to accomplish so much. You know what resonates with you and are able to make choices from a grounded place. When challenges arise, instead of agonizing about life's choices, you will feel like you can gracefully navigate and live joyously.

How would it feel to live a life of truth — to really show up every day the way you truly are, letting your spirit shine? How would it feel to be inspired, self-loving and complete, no matter what anyone says or does, or who agrees with you?

The answer is … amazing!

You can go through the motions of living: get up every day, go to a job you don't like; come home; watch TV; go to sleep; wake up and do it all over again … or you can decide you are going to do something really amazing that fulfills your soul's whole reason for being here.

Why Are You Here?

What is your spiritual responsibility? Do you know? In other words, how are you making this world better by being here, and what are you contributing? We are all on this earth for a reason. As I said, all of us are technically living, but not all of us are really doing something with our lives. You can live here and do nothing, or you can do something really amazing! (And if you are reading this, you are clearly invested in doing the latter!)

Ask yourself what the spirit inside your soul is telling you to do, and it will give you the answer. We all come here with a purpose, which we can fine tune by connecting to all the 5 Star Points within and without. Like I say in my song, "Pledge to Love You," "I believe we come here/to learn, share, express."

My spirit drives me to do everything I do. When my body is tired, it forces me to get up. Sometimes it forces me to stay up all night and morning to complete what I need to complete in order to continue to fulfill my life's purpose. I completely trust my spirit, and I allow it to have its way with my body, so I can allow my light to shine, with nothing to get in the way of its brightness! Are you holding your spirit back? (Just think about it!)

Go Back to the Birth of Your Spirit

I often say I do everything from a heart or spirit and mind connection. I find that there is great strength in thinking things through while connecting through your heart. You simply allow your spirit to shine through and your mind to take you through the steps that will allow you to understand what your spirit just cannot wait for you to accomplish! We can have dreams, and we can know our life's purpose, but sometimes we have to go back to where our spirits began and take steps so that are dreams can manifest with grace.

Here are a couple scenarios for you: A little girl that dreams of being a dancer on Broadway and showing up on TV and in films will get none of that accomplished if she continues to dream, but does not take classes, learn more about dance, and take the necessary steps to fulfilling her dream. A little boy who loves to sing and wants to put an album out, but does not think the process through and create a blueprint to achieve his goal is also not likely to end up standing proudly with a well-made, beautiful CD in his hand to share with the world.

Our spirit can tell us about our dreams here and there and may even spark some creative ideas, but it is our mind that allows the spirit to manifest. The mind is the ally and partner that lets us think our ideas through and bring them to fruition.

When creative people miss this important concept, they can really get into trouble. They wonder what they are supposed to do in their industry. They just want to sing, dance, write, draw, paint, play an instrument, or do their thing, but they do not think about the business and using their mind to work through the vision and bring the vision to life.

And sometimes the disconnect comes from not being able to figure out how to connect to their spirit – or to their inner peace and joy – in order to formulate the action steps that will lead them to success.

Have you seen your inner child lately?
Many people like to go back and reminisce about their childhood, because they feel great joy remembering the time when they were genuinely free. They did not know judgment, and they did what came naturally. In order to strengthen our spirit, we need to look back at that time when things were natural, organic and free, to connect to that little girl or boy that lived life abundantly, before being jaded by life's dark experiences and fears of what others might think of us … to go back to that space where we were unburdened and unafraid … where we could just "be."

Here is my own inner child story.

Ever since I was very small, I have always been very excited about the world and interested in getting into all kinds of adventures. But when I was growing up, because there were many that were not as energetic or excited as I was about living, I had very few people to share my dreams with. My brother was one of the few people as engaged in creating things that were out of this world as I was, so we were able to bond in a special way. I was never alone!

But I know there are a lot of kids who are not so lucky and do not have this extra ray of sunshine in their home; they have to keep their light shining all by themselves, and that can be a challenge.

As much as I did stand out, sometimes I wanted to hold back, because it seemed at times that blending in was the best thing to do. I wanted to fit in, and I didn't want to offend anyone. As a kid, I was surrounded by a lot of people that constantly talked about bad times and often competed with each other over negative aspects of their lives. For example, they would argue over who lived in the worst neighborhood or who had experienced the most hardship.

Even though I did not come from a rich family and had some truly tough times (that I still remember well!), I was a pretty happy and spunky kid. Still, being around all those depressed and unhappy people sometimes filled me with anxiety: I thought if I shined too bright and let my spirit loose, these people might not like me.

One of my most powerful memories is going to church as a child and hearing my elders ask members of the congregation, "How are you doing?" They usually responded by complaining about what they did not have or what a hard time they were having:

- ★ "I'm hanging in there."
- ★ "I'm alright."
- ★ "I'm not going to complain, but I could be doing better."
- ★ "I would be better if I could just find a way to make more money."
- ★ "I'm okay, but I have this pain."
- ★ It was very rare I would hear someone say, "I am simply fantastic."

I found myself copying these people's attitudes and saying some of the things they were saying when someone asked about how my spirit was. I would sometimes say, "I'm cool," or "I'm all right," even when I was doing well, great or even totally fabulous!

As I got older, I started to own who I was much more often. If I felt fabulous, I shouted about it. I noticed sometimes my energy would catch people off guard, but it ultimately brightened their day. Surprise! Positivity is just as infectious as negativity!

So, the theory I sometimes believed when I was younger, which I even touched on a little bit earlier in this book – that you have to blend in and hide your light in order to make others who are living in a grey or dark space more comfortable – was all wrong. If you just focus on being "you" – that little girl or boy you once were, in love with the world and your experiences – and sharing and celebrating your many gifts, you might be able to raise the vibration of the people around you.

When you share your positive attitude with people around you, you could possibly be changing lives, or planting a seed of this 5 Star Points philosophy that will continue to grow and help them move closer to happiness. And it will make you want to shine even brighter!

I am so grateful I stopped backing off and owned who I am. When I fully stepped into my own mind, body, spirit, emotions and environment, my life completely changed. My energy took on a life of its own!

Let your inner child shine!
You are and have always been you. Trust yourself! What are you afraid to say about yourself? What is an incredible talent you have that you have always wanted to develop, but were too afraid to pursue?

Please, please, please do not let that fabulous talent go to waste! I have seen some people accomplish some amazing feats that I would never imagine, and people who are hiding supernatural talent in favor of taking a job they hate that makes them miserable. Why would you hide your light?

Give your inner child permission to be happy ... and then let that child loose! Honor your root spirit, go for it, and really do it! Trust your authentic self and co-create with your spirit and with God to make great things happen.

Once you give that child free rein, you can work towards building your talent into a career that will embody your life's true purpose. Can you imagine never actually "working" a day in your life? When you connect with your raw spirit, you get to do what you love and get paid well for it!

Protect Your Spirit and Move into the Light
As connected as I feel now to all the 5 Star Points, sometimes I have found myself in a situation where I let negative energy creep in, potentially threatening to hold me back from fulfilling my life's purpose.

Have you ever felt like you were succumbing to negative energy on a daily, weekly or monthly basis and unable to focus on the light and on life's joy? When I have found myself stuck in that place, it has brought me down. I strive to manifest all the good things I know are inside me, but once again, the distractions can be thick and deep and emotionally embedded in my soul.

We must be careful that we do not allow dark, depressing energy to get ahold of us.
This energy often comes from negative thoughts, physical breakdowns, emotional breakdowns, depression and environmental darkness that can try to break our spirits. But we cannot let it!

Your spirit is powerful and you can absolutely push through the darkness in order to find something better. Do not allow for misery to set in. Be strong. I know from experience that sometimes giving in to bad habits can feel GREAT, but be careful of that temporary satisfaction; that moment of bliss can lead to a lifetime of pain and struggle, incompletion and breakdown with no achievement. You will awake up in a negative space with nothing accomplished and wonder, "Why did I stray from my path?"

In the past when I found myself stuck in that place, I recognized it really brought me down. I knew I could have been acting more positively and taking care of myself better, but I felt terrible. And on top of it, I had to get up and try to create, which normally brings me so much joy. When I give in to darkness, I am left empty, and I know I have so much more to offer.

We have all heard so many people tell stories like this – that something has a hold on them and is possessing them to engage in behaviors that do not reflect what is truly in their hearts and that are not good for them. Learning how to move from this darkness into the light and learning we are worth more than the things we do to destroy our bodies, minds and hearts and compromise the sanctity of the mind-body-spirit-emotions-environment connection is a process many of us have to go through. But you have to know: If you continue to engage in these activities, your road will not lead to a beautiful place full of light and happiness.

Food addiction, alcohol and drug addiction, sex addiction or holding onto partners or friends that keep you trapped in a dark space all hold your spirit back and prevent you from manifesting your dreams. But do not fret. All is not lost!

Even in that dark space, you are so close to getting on the path towards living the life you want. The only thing stopping you is your unwillingness to take part in activities that sweep you away and distract you from spreading your ray of light.

You have to protect that spirit of yours! It is easy to get into negative situations without even realizing how we got there. What seems like days can turn into weeks, months or years. Your mind and spirit say, "How did I waste a whole year thinking this way/being in this condition/being with this person? That is NOT the energy I want or need!"

If you feel your spirit is being sucked dry, you have the power to cut off the source of the drain! Hating where you are is not the answer; it just adds negative fuel to an already out-of-control fire. You must take action!

What are you doing to hurt your growth and development?

You might say you want to save money to do something special for yourself or build a business, but if you are out every night spending all your money, this is not helping you achieve your goal. If you are a musician, you might say you want to be healthy so you can perform at your best. But then you do not sleep or eat right, you use drugs, alcohol or stay out late every night partying, and your look, your voice or the art of movement in dance leaves you because you are not taking care of your instrument and your temple.

Is any of this mess described above really worth it?

If you are allowing yourself to get stuck in a rut of negative behaviors and not protecting your spirit, you have to face reality: You are killing the very thing you have been blessed with – YOURSELF. Your talents can't shine if you are on a dark path. Make some difficult decisions about life and decide to protect your spirit so you can be the best you can possibly be and stay the course towards living your life's purpose with no regrets!

Fall in Love with Yourself

You have probably heard this one before, but let it really sink in: How you treat yourself is how others will treat you. And you are closer to spirit when you are closer to self. Life really is an emanation of you. This is why you need to open your eyes and your heart and say what you want out loud. You can have it all!

Sometimes if you just show up, great things can happen. Showing up is a great first step, and showing up for yourself is imperative.

Break up with your story and learn to love yourself again. Maybe it served to protect you at one time, but how's it working for you now? People truly mirror how you relate to yourself, so start telling yourself that whatever happened is in the past. Events are neutral, and your whole life can change when you alter your perceptions!

Heal Your 5 Star Points

You need to heal the wounds of your mind, body, emotions and environment to allow your spirit to be free. As you gain more experience and start to mend your mind-body-spirit-emotions-environment connection, all the information you have about situations, people and events will reveal itself, as will the timing in which you will use it. Your intuition will start to kick into high gear, and you will be able to move forward with confidence.

Access your intuition, and forgive yourself!

Once you access the intuition that allows you to hear your spirit's voice, you must forgive yourself for the wrongs of your life. You may see them as "mistakes," but they got you where you are, and turned you into you!

Once you forgive, you can love wherever you go. The more you love, the more sacred each step will be. When you forgive yourself and embrace your spirit, you will step into your authentic self, be transformed and be capable of transforming people around you.

Warning: Forgiving yourself and stepping into your spirit will make you vulnerable!

But, great news! Vulnerability actually increases your power. Many see it as a weakness, but exposing your realness actually opens your heart and can allow you to deeply connect with yourself and others.

What are you afraid of? That people will not like you if you are authentic?

Is it better to be a lawyer or a doctor when what you really want to do is be a painter, because that is what your parents, friends or your significant other think you should do? Is it better to stay in a job or in a relationship because you think it will prevent you from losing a lot of money or your status, even though you are not happy?

Absolutely not!

Remember that when you first start this new journey towards living your life's purpose, you are a small seed that has everything to make a fruitful tree, so forgive your past darknesses and start to grow. You will make even more seeds and create groves upon groves of new, amazing trees.

Move into a Space of Acceptance

As soon as you move into the space where you are accepting your true self and pursuing your dreams, your energy will shift, and your spirit will enter in; you will no longer be busy doubting self and blocking yourself from being you. But how do you get into that accepting, loving place?

★ Be in a place to see the opportunity. If you are distracted by internal and external forces that are so convoluted they are causing a mess in your life, you may miss a sparkling opportunity because you will not even be able to see it.

★ Know what to do when an opportunity presents itself. Take advantage of it by taking the proper steps to allow for that opportunity to be a blessing then see how you can make it snowball into something magnificent!

From darkness comes light!

As clearly as I can see the positive and light in the world and as much as I focus on it to feed my spirit and generate high vibrations, the truth is, I see the darkness too and am aware that darkness and light must both exist in order to create balance. Still, I have played on both sides of the tracks, and the light is what I have chosen for myself.

People in the world can bring you down, but why focus on that? Be aware and be smart, then focus on your spirit and everything you are doing with your life. When you think of the world as a half-full cup, you will be able to bring positive experiences into your life and manifest your dreams.

Out with the old, dark things, and in with the new, bright things!

Turn issues into blessings.

Do you feel like you are constantly being confronted by "issues"? Well, every time you resolve a problem or clear up an issue on the inside, you make room for more blessings. You are not filled with the darkness and negativity, but instead, making room for light, loving and creative forces to swirl and make something fabulous happen.

Getting rid of issues is a form of detox, so beware! If you are not used to the process of clearing out toxins, I will tell you that sometimes during detox, you will feel worse before you feel better. Hang in there! It is all about reprogramming and laying a new foundation, so do not give up! And remember – all that renovation you are doing on the inside will show outwardly, attracting the best people, places and things to you.

Many people freak out when they get into an uncomfortable zone that they are not familiar with, and it causes them to give up and give into the fear and resistance. Stick with it! When you are connected with your spirit, you will feel like you. You will not have to fix or change anything, and you will be able to just be"!

Spirit Exercise #1: Connecting with your Childlike Spirit

Going back in time and meditating on a more uninhibited version of yourself can help you start to connect with your spirit so you can start being you and living your life's purpose. Below is a two-part exercise to help you connect with your inner child.

- ★ *Meditate on a specific time in childhood when you felt really hopeful about accomplishing a goal, and you went after it and succeeded. Write down how the outcome felt.*

- ★ *Think about 2-3 major goals you want to achieve in your life, and write down how you will feel when you get to the finish line. If you have already accomplished one of your dreams, be sure to write that down too!*

Here is what I came up with when I did this exercise.

Childhood Goal: I want to make music for people that expresses the joy I feel inside!

What I see, what I feel: I see myself on the backyard porch with my orange stick, singing "Saving All My Love for You" by Whitney Houston, my hair in two fluffy ponytails and wearing a white dress with a red ribbon. I am singing to the whole neighborhood, whether they liked it or not – loud, strong, powerful with so much joy and no care in the world. I am doing it because I love it, and no one can stop me!

I see myself sitting at my aunt's piano, not knowing one chord from the next, getting better and better every day, playing my heart out and making up songs on the spot that express my spirit and bring other people joy and happiness.

I see myself making up silly jingles in my room and in the kitchen with my brother, creating theme songs for cartoons.

Adulthood Goal: I want to make music that expresses my joy, music that the whole world will hear!

What I see, what I want, what I feel: There I am today, singing the same Whitney Houston song with the same enthusiasm, passion and love, but now with the real world experience to back it up and make it my reality.

There I am today, on set for the Dolly Parton and Queen Latifah, working on promotions for the movie *Joyful Noise*, getting hired to do a big music job for Warner Bros.

There I am today, writing the theme song for the cartoon "Shelly's Adventures," doing voiceovers and writing and singing jingles for radio shows and commercials for products.

What does your little boy or girl want? I had to make music because it was my way to be able to express my spirit. It could not just be a hobby; it had to be my life, much as helping people and writing this book had to be part of my mission and purpose. It is the only way for me to live authentically and express my spirit!

Spirit Exercise #2: Affirmations about Your Spirit.
Tell your spirit you want it to come out and play by making a commitment to pursue the dreams that align with your life's purpose through daily spirit affirmations. Keep saying them, and feel a better connection to your spirit. Watch your dreams come true!

> ★ *Make a list of affirmations about your spirit. Don't forget to say your "I am"s!*

Here are some sample affirmations to inspire you.

- ★ I am acknowledging spirit and allowing for magic to appear.
- ★ I am committing to myself and who I am while I am taking action steps.
- ★ I am allowing for abundance to come into my life.
- ★ I am grateful for my gift of life and all additional gifts I am receiving.

★ I am performing gracefully and powerfully commanding the stage with strong vocals, giving the people a fantastic and divine experience.

Spirit Exercise #3: Gratitude Journal

What are you grateful for? There is a Chinese proverb that states, "Gratitude is the open door to abundance." While this showed up one day in a simple fortune cookie, it was the most important quote I think I have ever read in my life. Creating a gratitude journal and writing in it every night can help you focus on the most positive and important elements of your life so you reprogram your life and better connect with your spirit and all the 5 Star Points. It also helps you learn how to search for the diamonds in the rough of your life, open up your heart and attract more sparkling opportunities. You will be exhilarated when you start sensing your vibrations rise!

Write down 5 things you are grateful for each night.

Tips for keeping a gratitude journal:

1. Take stock of the little and big things that made you particularly happy today.
2. Describe how the joyful events of your day made your spirit feel.
3. Give thanks to the people in your life who brightened your experience today and made you feel most like your authentic self.

Nurturing Your Spirit: Accountability Chart

Use this chart to track the progress you make strengthening your connection to your SPIRIT each month. Put self-nurturing activities you engage in that support your spirit on the left-hand side, and every day you focus on the activities listed, give yourself a check mark!

ACCOUNTABILITY CHART

I am nuturing my spirit this month by...

Example: Writing an entry in my gratitude journal

	M	T	W	Th	F	S	Su	M	T	W	Th	F	S	Su	M	T	W	Th	F	S	Su	M	T	W	Th	F	S	Su

CHAPTER 5

Ignite Your Electrifying EMOTIONS

"I don't want to be at the mercy of my emotions. I want to use them, to enjoy them, and to dominate them." **– Oscar Wilde**

Emotions are our allies. One of life's greatest gifts is the ability to feel emotion, TRUE emotion. Whether elation or sadness, emotions let us know we are alive, that we FEEL. The ability to feel emotion is something we as human beings on this earth all share, and it makes us mighty and strong. We experience many emotions in life. Some, of course, are more enjoyable than others!

It's easy to accept the feelings of joy that come to us. Those moments of happiness are felt in the depth of our soul, and we celebrate them. Each of us has different things in our life that may bring those feelings to light. Happiness can come in those day to day moments from things like sharing great conversation with a friend, a hug from a child, from a job well done. And there are those "life's amazing, one of a kind" moments which will live forever in your heart, whether the birth of a child, learning that you got that perfect job you were waiting to hear about, sharing a glance with your love or completing a major heartfelt project you have been working on. The emotion of joy is not one that we fight. We treasure those feelings and bask in their glow!

And then, there are the feelings of sadness. Not as easy to accept, are they? But let's face it, life isn't perfect. While we welcome joy in whole-heartedly, many times we may try to fight the emotion of sadness, trying to block it out, push it away, ignore it. But my friend, in those moments in life where sadness comes, accept it. Face it, explore it, and then you will be able to move on. And move on you will!

Many times, we cannot figure out what is ailing us, because we are so emotionally numb. The point in time when I get really excited while working with clients is when they are crying and what others might call "emotional." Why? Because that is when I can help them connect to what is really going on inside and allow them to ride the wave of truth to what is affecting them. When you are in this heightened emotional state, you are feeling, on the brink of journeying into your authentic spirit, about to unlock a previously hidden part of your mind/spirit, connect to it and confront it so you can move forward.

Your Emotions are Yours and Yours Alone
Keep in mind your emotions are *your* emotions. We need to be careful about emotions that pop up as a result of someone else's actions. I'm pretty sure you know what I mean, but allow me to explain! You heard that someone said a hurtful thing about you, and now you feel horrible. You sit and think about it, you obsess over it, you feel sad, you search and search within yourself to figure out what you did.

You know what?! This wheel-spinning activity is not worth the precious time you have here on earth! Don't let someone else control your emotions. YOU and you alone control how you react or respond to something. We only have one life to live, so don't let anyone else dictate the type of emotions you will feel.

And also, remember that emotions are something that let you experience life fully. Don't be ashamed to laugh out loud with joy, cry in times of sorrow, scream into a pillow when you feel angry. Be the person you are. Emotions are beautiful and allow us to feel and celebrate that we are alive. You are lucky to be alive and to be able to feel so powerfully about your experiences!

Emotions are Pure Energy
Your emotions are containers for boundless energy – physical, heartfelt and psychological – and when you discover your mission, purpose and

intention, you will be able to tap into that energy and use it to build a rock-solid foundation rooted in the 5 Star Points.

To get a sense of the energy emotions produce, think about a major issue you are having right now in your life, then go into your heart and listen to what it is telling you about it. Perhaps you are miserable at work, and you are trying to decide whether to stay or to go. What are the facts in the situation? How does it make you feel? Is it affecting your mind, body, spirit, emotions and environment? All this information adds up into positive, kinetic energy that can help you move forward and solve the problem.

Of course, it is one thing to have a lot of information about a challenge you are facing, and another to integrate that information into your consciousness so you can take action and move forward. How you relate to yourself as you are overcoming the obstacle is the real issue at play.

You need to take a look deep within yourself and make sense of how you are treating yourself as you work towards a solution and a way to get back on track to living your life's purpose.

The Haves and the Have Nots

As you continue on the road towards an improved relationship with yourself and your emotions that allows you to pursue your dreams with dedication and enthusiasm, you need to get creative. Stop complaining about what you do not have and what is not working ... and focus on the goal you want to achieve!

Aren't you a creative person? Well, then hop to it! Create a list of possible outcomes for your life and focus on the most positive. You can change your entire attitude when you look your emotions in the eye and process how you feel about your situation. Converting your emotions into thoughts and physical action steps is possible! When the decisions you make are entrenched in the 5 Star Points and moving you closer to your dream, you can accomplish anything.

Emotions are a choice.

Have you ever caught yourself saying, "I had no choice" when explaining why you settled for an outcome that made you feel rotten and unfulfilled inside? I hear someone say this almost every day. People who make this statement a lot complain about how they are stuck in a dead-end job, a relationship that does not fulfill them, or are unable to make that leap to manifest their dreams, claiming they have no options, that the world is completely closed to them, that everyone is against them, conspiring to drag them down and make them miserable. Do you know one of these Negative Nancys or Neds who is always upset, always sad and pessimistic, always outraged, always the victim of foul play? One of these Negative Nancys or Neds may even be so skilled at explaining the wrongdoings that you start to believe she/he is really onto something and actually is the unluckiest person on the planet.

Negative emotions are just as contagious as positive emotions, and vice versa! Often, all these pessimistic people want is for their emotions to be acknowledged, and to let others know they are in pain. They are at the mercy of their spinning, tumultuous emotions, and they do not know how to make it over to the sunny side of the street, because their mind-body-spirit-emotions-environment connection has been severed. Thankfully, it is never too late to take charge of your emotions or any part of your inner or outer self.

The truth is you always have a choice, and your power to choose makes you extremely powerful. Even if the world seems to be crashing down around you, you are a human being with consciousness and you can choose to feel your own emotions every day. You can also choose to be a victim, or choose to overcome the chaos by empowering yourself on all levels to achieve exactly what you want in your life. We do not see the world objectively, as it actually is; how we perceive it is largely based on the emotions that are going on inside us. Just remembering that can help you create a brighter reality that encourages you to be bold, courageous, grateful and joyful.

Your Emotions are Thoughts that You Feel

So many of us have been conditioned to mistake the gist of the following statement for truth: "Emotions come from an irrational place, and thoughts come from a rational place." We are constantly told that there is a war going on between the fly-by-night emotions we feel in our hearts and the "sensible" thoughts we have in our heads. We are often told that making decisions based on our emotions is irresponsible – that our emotions bubble up from a place of weakness. As a result, we are often afraid to express our feelings, or to take risks based on gut feelings and our intuition.

The concept that your mind and your emotions are in a constant battle is simply not true! In fact, your emotions and your mind are harmoniously connected. Emotions are thoughts that you feel. And if you are not making decisions about your life's purpose with your whole being – your mind, your body, your emotions, your spirit, and the environment inside you – you are missing important information that can help you completely change your life for the better.

Surf the emotional wave!

When we are connected to all our emotions, we can ride the waves right back to the root of the issue that is causing us to struggle. And by going back to the beginning, we can get valuable insight into ...

★ What is holding us back.

★ What is blocking our progress.

★ Why we feel so hurt and angry so often.

★ Why we keep sabotaging ourselves.

★ Why we are terrified.

★ Why we are judging ourselves.

★ Much, much more!

Whatever thoughts we have cycling inside of us come out when we face our emotions head on, and often times we discover our problem is that we are allowing negative, self-effacing thoughts and emotions to creep in and compromise the life, career and relationships we thought we were actively building. When you are operating in a negative space, you will not be able to do your best work, or to create beauty for yourself and others. These rogue emotions will hinder you and hinder your progress, leading us to harmful behavior that will make us lash out with intense feelings that can dirty everything we do.

On the other hand, when we ride the wave of our emotions, we can discover an abundance of loving, heartwarming emotions teeming with high-frequency energy that can push us into a positive place and push us into a positive, joyful zone. These emotions will support you as you work on your connection to your authentic self and move into your full radiance.

Are you paralyzed by emotional fear?
Emotions can be full of electrifying energy that set your soul on fire ... but they can also be dramatic, haunting and hurtful in a way that can completely paralyze you. It is these second types of emotions that can really frighten us with their power, turn into chaos, tempt us to hit "stop" and decide we cannot live our dreams. We may feel we are being ripped apart, and we may feel we do not have a clue how to stop it or how to get to a safe and peaceful place again.

Remember what I said before? Fear is a dream crusher! When you feel fear about anything – your mind, your body, your spirit, your emotions or your environment – you will feel unsafe, and you will not be able to continue. Fear will level your bravery and send you running back to old habits that make you *feel* safe because they are familiar, but do not actually contribute to fulfilling your life's purpose.

You can either be your own tyrant ... or your own savior!
I want to reassure you: There is nothing wrong with being "emotional." It is how you perceive your emotions and use them, and what you find out about yourself and your calling through this process that will help keep you in alignment and focused on the prize: Your new life focused on everything you love, full of endless possibilities! Your emotions can make you a slave to your own uncertainty and fear or they can save your life and help you shine.

Sometimes when I watch an artist singing powerful songs with moving lyrics, I break down in tears – not because I am dismayed, sad or depressed, but because I can actually feel this person's spirit, soul and emotions in my own heart. My father's favorite song was "A Change is Gonna Come" by Sam Cooke. After my father died, I sat and listened to this record over and over again, and I felt completely moved by every note and element of the song. My feelings could not be contained, and I let them flow freely.

The poignant emotions I felt listening to this song in this moment told me I absolutely had to cover "A Change is Gonna Come," record it and include it as part of my Spirit of Oya album, dedicated to him. And it was also the feelings I was having in this special moment that encouraged me to complete my album. This song was a part of my spirit and my soul, and I had to share it with others.

Before this event, I had always loved the song, but after my father's death, the energy behind it was even more powerful. I could feel the push of my Father's spirit and even my late Grandmother's spirit nudging me to move forward and live my dream of being a bona fide solo recording artist. While I was emotional about my father's death, my emotions reminded me why I am here, and that before I left this earth, I must share my gift and fully commit to the reason I was brought to this very place on earth.

Why did I feel this motivation, even in a space of deep pain and loss? Because I realized it would even more painful not to stick to my guns, create my CD and live and breathe one of my most heartfelt dreams. In this profound emotional space, listening to Sam Cooke's voice, thinking of my father's love, I owned my life. I could touch, taste, feel, smell and hear my life unfolding in front of me through this song.

- ★ I saw myself in the studio recording with top-notch musicians.
- ★ I saw myself performing in front of thousands, making enough money to support myself and then some, by following my own, crazy and beautiful dream.
- ★ I saw my music touching people around the world.

I knew I had to follow my emotions. I followed them right into the studio and let them take the wheel and guide the project, supported by all the other 5 Star Points that had been awakened in me.

While for this project, I did use my emotions to guide me, it was not a melodramatic scene. I acknowledge my emotions and integrated them into my business mind, physically took action, created the proper environment and allowed my emotions to connect to my purpose and allow my spirit to come forth and co-create. It was my emotions and my humanity that took me back to the heart of who I am.

I was empowered! I could see myself, and knew I was operating from a space of true love. I was honoring, loving and respecting myself and my talents. I heard the calling, and off I went!

Your feelings will not be ignored until you act on them.
When our emotions and our calling come knocking, we cannot ignore them! We must listen to our "gut instincts" and those pangs we get when we are not doing what we most want to do with our lives. If you have not felt any of that yet, you will! When you start to connect with your emotions, you will know that feeling the second you have it. You might even feel physical pain when you realize you are not fully sharing who you are. And then you will know for certain that you cannot dim your light anymore!

I am sure you know people who continue to drudge through a job they hate, and they cannot stop thinking about it, but they also do not seem to want to get out of their own way. Statements like "I don't even like this stupid job," "I don't want to do this nonsense" are their regular refrains. And they are lashing out at anyone within earshot, blaming their boss for their erratic, negative outbursts.

If you are hiding from your emotions and ignoring your spirit's need to create in this manner, the second you make a connection with your-self, you will hurt. Yes. You will hurt, and it will probably make you feel confused, overwhelmed and generally unpleasant, and you will want to run out of that space as fast as you can! The instant you feel this urge to flee, I encourage you to stay and fight! Take action, confront your painful emotions and use the valuable information you uncover about yourself through this process in order to devise a plan and take action steps to come back into the light and live your life well!

Choose not to Be Overwhelmed by Your Emotions

I said this already, but it bears repeating: Your life is full of choices, and you are the powerful decision maker. And the choices you make will determine the course of your life.

Remember what I said earlier in this book about steering clear of getting overwhelmed? Well, that advice applies to your connection to your emotions too! Being overwhelmed by your feelings is a choice. You can panic, or you can take charge and CHOOSE not to let your emotions overtake you. There's that power of choice again! You have it! Even if you are willing to make changes in your life, you can still feel unmotivated to actually manifest your dreams and participate in the authentic flow of your life.

Easy does it!

When you get in that place of emotional overwhelm, accept you have momentarily lost your way, sit quietly and let your own story reveal itself to you. Sometimes we have to sit in the "not knowing" energy to come into ourselves and find the knowing energy to embrace our emotions and let them lead us back to our intended path.

Maybe you have been confused before; maybe you are currently confused about what you are feeling and cannot find an escape plan that takes us back to the main road of your destiny. No matter what happens, when we feel bewildered by our emotions, we must resist shutting down and getting stubborn, allowing ourselves to avoid feeling. Keep an open mind, and dive into your heart and really listen!

Make listening one of your best skills.

Listening is probably one of the most important skills you can develop in your personal and professional life. First of all, no matter what industry we are in, we all need to listen to our clients and what they want so we can use our gifts to fulfill their needs. When your clients come to you, I encourage you to listen to them and also for clues that tell you what they want and how you can help them manifest what they want. Most clients just want to be heard, and when they feel heard and know you care, you win them over! You have a client for life.

Listening is a "skill," so you have to actively work on it. The development of really fabulous listening skills just does not happen magically! They cannot be contrived. You have to really care, and I absolutely want you to learn to access your caring, empathetic emotions! When you care, you really become a part of the project this new client or collaborator is asking you to join. You both feel that you are invested, secure with each other and on the same page.

Listen to yourself.

Without *your* emotions and all the other elements of the 5 Star Points in play inside an all around you, this dream of yours is not going to work. You are the most important person in your life. Are you a caretaker type, always putting everyone else's thoughts, feelings and needs before your own? Many of us have been taught our whole lives that this practice of taking care of everyone else before ourselves is noble, that pure selflessness is to be admired and celebrated.

We need to reprogram ourselves to realize that we cannot truly care for anyone else unless we are putting ourselves first. We cannot respond to the emotional and physical needs of others until we have listened to and heard ourselves and feel connected and responsible for our own needs. Blindly putting others' needs before our own is neither admirable nor responsible.

I am not saying, "Be selfish" or "Be egotistical." Absolutely not! We are all in this life on earth as vibrant, engaged beings together, so we need to listen to each other and respect others. I am simply saying that you must listen to yourself first and be aware of your emotions and what you need in your life. The answers to living a full-engaged and joyful life in which all your dreams come true are right there within you. Listen to these voices, and live your life's purpose! And when you really hear them, trust them and trust yourself in order to have healthy personal and business relationships that will bring you great fulfillment.

Connect Emotionally with Your Purpose and Mission

Hopefully by now you have been taking some time to think about your mission and purpose. Do you know what it is? Check in with it, think about it and really be with it for a while. Now, think about how your mission and purpose makes you feel deep down inside. Can you feel that?

Chances are, when I asked you to come up with a mission and purpose, you looked at this mission very objectively. You thought about it with your mind, but did not let yourself feel it with your emotions. Don't worry: This is not entirely your fault ... but you do need to change your approach immediately in order to fully connect to this mission and take the proper action steps to making it happen. Many of us are trained not to make decisions and life plans with our heartfelt feelings, when setting goals, we sometimes forget to consider the emotions attached to them. For many, this is just an unconscious way we protect ourselves from fear and disappointment, or maybe those people who have told you to "stop being so emotional" made you feel you did not have permission to let your feelings have their say.

Check in with your mission and purpose regularly to center yourself and overcome any negative or overwhelming emotions. Remember that your emotions will not be ignored! And if you are not connected to them, they can wreak havoc on your mind, body, spirit and environment until you let them speak to you. They will compromise forward progress in your life if you do not call on them when they raise their hands.

Sometimes you will feel you have too much going on inside and outside to access your emotions. But the truth comes out when we connect with our emotions. When you get too "mental" and push them down, you lose the powerful juice you need to forge ahead.

Stay present to pass gracefully through pain.
As you are working on building a foundation based on the 5 Star Points system, there will be times when you feel pain or discomfort. This pain and discomfort might even feel so great you fear you will not be able to endure. Whenever you are making a revolutionary change to your way of being, there are bound to be major growing pains.

But please DO NOT GIVE UP.

Stay focused and heart centered. Check in with your mission, purpose and dream, and imagine how marvelous you will feel when your dreams come true, and all the parts of you click. The time when you will know from the top of your head to the tips of your toes that you are doing what you love and living your life's purpose is coming soon, so you can't give up now! If this process was easy, everyone would be doing it all the time. The fact that you are going through it right now means you are strong and capable, and that you can see it through to the end!

Any emotional pain you are feeling right now or in the future will pass. If you are not sure you believe me, let us go back to something attached to the body: working out. When you first start working out, sometimes you have soreness and pain from starting this major task of getting physically fit. But once you get into the groove, you are in the groove. And when you start seeing real results, staying on task becomes easier.

When pain arises, stay present and stay involved in the process. And please, stay loving to yourself! There will be twists and turns on the road to manifesting your dream. You may catch a nail or two or a bump, and you may even get a flat tire, but just know this is only a temporary setback – a pause. Work through it and get back to navigating yourself to your dream destination.

Forgive Your Emotional Judgments

We talked about forgiveness, but it is such an important action that I need to mention it again! Remember that self-forgiveness is only necessary when we have made a judgment. Many of us judge ourselves for our emotions, but when it comes to your emotions, none of them are "wrong." Why are you judging your legitimate feelings?

Some of us feel "embarrassed" when we have strong emotions. But much of this feeling of embarrassment is based in concern over what others will think of the way you feel or how your emotions will make others feel. I repeat: Your emotions are yours and yours alone! I encourage you to forgive your emotional judgments and stop worrying about how others perceive your emotions.

When you forgive yourself, you will feel the energy shift and the weight release, and you will be free to feel even more deeply than ever before and connect powerfully with your emotions. When you clear up an issue in your life and really let go of it, the next time a similar issue comes to you, you will be able to react from a place of peace and clear up the issue much faster than before. When you are grounded, you learn to respond instead of react.

Forgive your judgments to increase the strength of your foundation and increase the love you have for yourself, so you can move to a higher state of consciousness. The higher your level of consciousness, the less concerned you will be about who likes you and what others think. This emotional, mental, spiritual clutter will fall away, and you will be able to concentrate on what is most important: living your dream!

Let feelings rise up and out!

I encourage you to let even the feelings associated with troubling events come up and out. There is an inherent wisdom inside of you that knows where you are at emotionally at every given moment and can determine what you can handle and what you must do to get back into a place of alignment. Listen to this wisdom! Identify any judgments you have about yourself and release them as quickly as you can, then acknowledge your feelings and let them come out.

When you make what you perceive as a "mistake," resist beating yourself up! The ability to learn from every situation and use the information we have to understand the actions we can do differently in the future and improve our lives going forward is what makes human being exceptional and wise. "Messing up" from time to time is really OK, as long as you learn. In fact, making mistakes is a necessary part of human growth and development!

Many of us obsess over mistakes we have made in the past, when the issue is either completely resolved or actively resolving. Why waste the energy on this practice? Instead, take action steps to allow yourself to move forward:

Look at the mistake you made and see why you still have pain surrounding it.

Examine this so-called mistake more closely and acknowledge what you can learn from it so you can actively heal the pain and release it.

Let go of past mistakes and accept that they are gone and done with, so you can get grounded, find peace and allow yourself to heal.

Remember those positive statements!

We need to continue to "accentuate the positive" and "eliminate the negative" if we want to forge ahead with our heartfelt dreams. I introduced that concept to you when I discussed the mind, and, since your emotions are thoughts that you feel, the same thing goes when it comes to connecting with your emotional center!

Emotions Exercise #1: Checking in with Your Mission, Purpose and Intentions

As I said, when you began formulating your mission, purpose and intentions earlier in this book, you may have kept it straightforward, objective and thoughts-oriented.

> ★ *Refine your mission, purpose and intentions by adding the emotions that are attached to your heartfelt dreams to the mix.*

I encourage you to get in touch with your emotions right now! How does the idea of fulfilling your dreams make you feel? Write it down!

Here are some examples:

- ★ "My intention is to write young adult novels that will be loved by teenagers worldwide. When I am holding my published book in my hand and knowing that young people are connecting with the words I have written, and I am able to support myself financially with my writing, I will feel great joy and happiness that will allow me to keep writing for my whole life."

- ★ "My intention is to run a production company focused on making wonderful documentaries that touch people's hearts around the world. When I am sitting in the theater at the premiere of my first film, watching an audience be moved by my work, I will be able to embrace their emotions and feel great joy that they are connecting with it."

It goes without saying, make sure you are starting your statements with "MY INTENTION IS," being clear and to the point about what you want and keeping all language positive.

Emotions Exercise #2: Self-Forgiveness

Are you in the habit of forgiving your judgments? If not, now is the time to start!

> ★ *Write down a list of 5 judgments you have made about yourself in the past month, and forgive yourself for them.*

This exercise may sound like a tall order, but if you want to get into the habit of not judging yourself, getting in alignment and manifesting your dreams, you need to forgive the judgments you have made (and continue to make) about yourself! How can you rewrite your story if you have not forgiven yourself?

For example ...

- ★ "I am a failure. I can't get anything done."
- ★ "I am not good enough."
- ★ "I get so angry with myself for crying when someone criticizes me about my work. That is such a weak thing to do. I need to stop being so thin skinned."

Tell yourself you have the right to feel your emotions and express them. Let go of judgments, rewrite your story and create your reality!

- ★ "I forgive myself for judging myself as a failure."
- ★ "I forgive myself for buying into the story that I am not good enough. The truth is my music teacher told me that, but I am really an amazing trumpet player."
- ★ "I forgive myself for judging myself as being so angry, weak and thin skinned. I forgive myself for judging myself as being weak for crying."

Love your work and yourself so much that judgments have no place in your life. Focus your energy on allowing your light to shine through your work and be OK with whatever judgments others will make. Do not let judgments distract you from displaying your work proudly and letting the world see you manifesting your dream and living your life's purpose!

Emotions Exercise #3: Affirmations about Your Emotions

Emotions are thoughts that you feel! That means we can easily create positive self-talk around our emotions.

> ★ *Create "I am" affirmations about your emotions to stay in the habit of positive self-talk.*

For example ...

- ★ I am acknowledging that my emotions are my allies.
- ★ I am gracefully riding the waves of my emotions to the truth of my heart and spirit connecting me to my dream and mission.
- ★ I am allowing my emotions to assist me creatively so I can pour out great creations.

Nurturing Your Emotions: Accountability Chart

Use this chart to track the progress you make getting in touch with your EMOTIONS each month. Put self-nurturing activities you engage in that tap into your emotions on the left-hand side, and every day you focus on the activities listed, give yourself a check mark!

ACCOUNTABILITY CHART

I am nuturing my emotions this month by...

Example: Forgiving my judgements about myself by writing postive "I am" affirmations about my emotions

	M	T	W	Th	F	S	Su	M	T	W	Th	F	S	Su	M	T	W	Th	F	S	Su	M	T	W	Th	F	S	Su

CHAPTER 6

Generate Your Peaceful ENVIRONMENT

"The first step toward success is taken when you refuse to be
a captive of the environment in which you first find yourself."
– Mark Caine

I want to take you on a short journey. Close your eyes and imagine your home. Picture yourself putting the key in the door, turning the key and walking in. Look straight ahead and to the left and right. Now, in your imagination, move through your home, through each room. Take in what it looks like, what it smells like, how each room makes you feel. Open your eyes and take a moment or two to take in those feelings. Absorb them into your soul so you can really, truly feel.

For the next part of the journey, I want you to do the same thing again, but with a little twist. Close your eyes, but now as you walk through your home, I want you to imagine how each room would look, smell and feel if it was exactly how you wanted it to be. I'm not talking about material things. I'm not talking about, "Oooh I wish I had that 60-inch big screen TV!" I'm talking about imagining what you want in the context of what you already have within you and in your environment, with no more than a little tweak here or there. Now open your eyes and do the same thing as before: Absorb these visions and how they make you feel in your soul.

Which of these two "visions" makes you feel better? And more importantly, which vision makes you feel more at home? After all, your home should make you feel comfortable and completely "at home." Your home should and can be a place that supports you and reminds you of where you want to go.

If you are feeling great and your vision and reality are the same, I'm elated! But if you are feeling as though your vision and your real home aren't in alignment, we have some work to do!

Your Home Must Bring You Joy

Your environment, and what you surround yourself with, what you look at every day, what you walk through in your hallways, and the pictures you look at should all make you feel joy. When our surroundings are a crazy mess, we cannot feel at peace. When we have items in our homes that remind us of something negative, how can we feel joy looking at them?

Your body is your temple, and your home is your sanctuary. Your home is the place where you should let out a sigh of relief when you walk in the door after a difficult day. It is a place where you must feel at peace. Hey, let's admit it: Not all of us are neat. But organization helps save us from the stress of trying to find missing things. We may not all love to clean, but doesn't it feel great to walk into a clean home, especially your *own* clean home? Think about that, and how you can take steps in the right direction.

So, in a loving way, I want to begin by challenging you to start taking steps to create that home environment you dream of – the one where you are surrounded by everything that makes you feel joyful, the things that make you want to be at your home, feel "at home" and at peace. Help your environment help you manifest all you want in life.

You and your home, together in perfect harmony!

You and your home must be harmonious. Throw out that you need to have a mansion. Where you are is where you are, and you can create your own ideal environment. You want a bigger and more lavish space, which is fine, but where you are today is what will take you to the next day, to the next month, to the next year and to the place and time where you can own the home that you wish for.

If you live in a small rental unit or room that you are renting, it is enough! We all have to start from somewhere! However, whining about your small space does nothing but take up valuable time. Please be thankful for the space that you have. It may sound like something your mother would tell you to make you appreciate what you have, but there really are people who do not even have a space. There are people who are homeless, so the fact that you are in your bedroom, living room, or somewhere else safe inside right now reading this book means that at the very least, you have a space. From that space, your life can and will start to blossom if you work the 5 Star Points System and believe in yourself, so just make sure you honor that space, in the same way you honor your body, the home inside which your spirit lives. Your home is the environment from which you create and become the best you can be. You will outgrow this space with wonderful creations. You will prosper and be able to move on, but now just give thanks and appreciate that you have a space to create.

Where Do You Actually Live?
When I was in high school, I started to read books on feng shui. I just thought it was interesting. I was not trying to be a feng shui practitioner I just found it interesting. One book led to another book, to another audio book, to another video. After researching the topic on the internet during grad school, I felt like there was more for me to learn.

At the time, I had come to the conclusion that the mind, body, spirit and emotions were the main points of focus for those of us who want to live out our dream. But after thinking about the concept of the body housing the spirit and considering the state of people's houses, I started to get more and more concerned about where we actually live. We live two places: in our bodies and in our homes. Our bodies are our homes, and our houses, apartments, condos or rooms – if you live at home with your parents or are renting a room or garage – we live in are also our homes. And they both must be taken care of. We must be in tune with all the places we reside.

As I continued to mull over the ideas of houses and homes, and the other 4 points of what would become the 5 Star Points system, I went back into my mental rolodex of the things I had studied and I was compelled to read more about feng shui. Eventually, I decided that the fact I had been interested in feng shui and the concepts surrounding it for so long probably meant I should formally study it. I searched and searched for a school that would be practical to my clients, because some of the feng shui that I had studied I knew would not reach my audience. In the United States many follow the Chinese modality of feng shui, and though I have always respected that modality tremendously, I knew my special take on feng shui would be beneficial to my clients and creative partners. I was confident that introducing the basic concepts to others in conjunction with the environmental affirmations I believe in so strongly would change their lives. (More on feng shui later in this chapter!)

Does your home and your neighborhood support the manifestation of your dreams?

The state of the neighborhood in which your spiritual and physical home is placed is important to your personal development, the mind-body-spirit-emotions-environment connection and your ability to manifest your dreams. Your neighborhood is where your "place" is placed and includes all the people, things and energies around you.

Is your home...

- ★ on a main street, in a high-traffic area?
- ★ on an out-of-the-way street in a quiet area where few cars and people pass?

Are the people you live with around you...

- ★ supportive of your dreams and in your energy flow?
- ★ constantly mid argument, spewing negative energy that drains you?

Are the things you have in your home ...

- ★ things that support your vision and help contribute to your ability to manifest your dreams?
- ★ things that remind you of negative experiences and people from your past or present?

Is your home set up...

- ★ so that positive, high-vibration energy can flow freely through your home?
- ★ so that energy feels stagnant and makes you feel stuck and dark?

Are the items around your home...

- ★ organized, so you can easily get them when you need to use them to support your life and creation?
- ★ disorganized, so you are constantly searching for things you need, distracting yourself from living your dream and creating?

In terms of the organization and cleanliness of your home...

- ★ Is your home clean and free of clutter, allowing you to feel open, happy and free to create and invite fellow creators over?
- ★ Is your home jumbled and messy, leaving you feeling trapped, overwhelmed and too ashamed of your space to invite over guests?

When it comes to the balance of elements in your home environment...

- ★ Is the light and energy "just right," leaving you feeling at ease and able to rest, relax and create with ease?
- ★ Is it very dark in your space or too bright...or do you sense more yin than yang as you are trying to "be"?

These are just a handful of key factors that are important to creating a harmonious environment to live, love and create in. With the above list in mind, where does your "place" stand?

Clear the clutter ... this time in your environment!

We greatly underestimate what a powerful effect clutter can have on our souls. Clutter can zap you mentally, physically, emotionally and spiritually and make you unhappy in your environment.

There are two types of clutter: physical and psychic. Physical clutter is easy to see. When our homes are physically cluttered, we can see the mess right before our eyes: clothes strewn about; magazines and newspapers stacked high; DVDs and CDs piled everywhere; stacks upon stacks of other items that do not fit in closets and thus remain in clear view, taking up space and making us feel overwhelmed by "stuff." Physical clutter is not our friend, and it can have serious effects on our mind-body-spirit-emotions-environment connection and our ability to create and live our life's purpose, so we need to clean it up and get organized if we want to manifest our dreams.

Psychic clutter can be a little more difficult to spot, but you can clean it up! We were already introduced to psychic clutter when we discussed the mind. Psychic clutter can begin in the physical world, and physical clutter can be a symptom of the psychic clutter inside ourselves. So how can we get rid of it?

You and Your Home Are Connected

Many people do not realize that you and your home are inextricably linked. The state of your home can reflect what is going on inside you and vice versa.

For example when I come into my home and I see clothes thrown all over the place I laugh. Why? Because I know better. When I start to see physical clutter, I know my life has descended into a bit of chaos. It usually happens when I am doing a lot of traveling, getting no rest and an all over the place. Things in my life and within me are not balanced, and my home sure shows it!

This is why when I go into my clients' homes, I can often tell what is going on in their lives before they even say a word. Case in point, I remember going into a couple's home to help them feng shui their space. It is my favorite feng shui story to date. The wife was a believer in feng shui, but her husband was not a believer when we began, and initially did not want to waste his time on the process.

The husband joined the wife and me on the tour of the house, and that was when something interesting happened. When I walked into the bedroom, his mind was on everything else, and I wondered what I could possibly say to engage him. He rolled his eyes and was totally not into anything I was saying until after I gently asked them if I could discuss anything with them: "How intimate is too intimate?" The wife immediately responded that she was open to anything I had to say. The husband shrugged his shoulders, barely listening to me until...

I asked them how their love life was, and if they felt like there was enough intimacy in their marriage. The wife immediately turned pink and said, "Oh no, we do not have to discuss that." But the husband, with lightning speed, turned his attention to me and asked me to repeat my question, which I did.

"Now we're talking!" he said. "There is not enough of that going on at all. What do you see, or what can we do about that?"

I smiled as professionally as I could. I wanted to fall on the floor laughing at how the husband had perked up at that moment, even though he was clearly very serious about what he was saying. Of course, I was also certainly there to help, and their problem was real and nothing to be ashamed of, so I moved forward with my professional consultation.

In truth, the couple had everything wrong with their bedroom. It was neither a sacred love sanctuary for intimacy nor even a place for good rest. You could barely move around. The vibe of the room was not fresh, happy and organized, but all over the place. Things were stacked up high. The night stands were not placed properly, as one was up against the wall and the other was lingering somewhere else entirely, taking away from the balance of the room. There were pictures of the whole family, including kids and the wife's father on the headboard. (Can you imagine having sex with your wife with your father-in-law and your kids looking on and smiling?! Better yet, how about stubbing your toe coming into the bedroom, or hitting your knee on the numerous items stacked up and killing the whole love-making vibe?)

In addition to the rest of this chaos, there was artwork that showed two people separated, looking sad and torn apart as if they had just broken up rather than artwork depicting two people together holding hands, two animals known to stay together for a lifetime, etc., creating a place where husband and wife can come together. This was, hands down, the worst room I had seen at that point. The bedroom is a place for husband and wife to come together, but this couple had a string of environmental affirmations destined to keep them apart.

Say, "Yes, yes, yes!" to environmental affirmations.

I am heavy on environmental affirmations. I use them all over my space. As a matter of fact, I invested in commissioning the wonderful artist Jemar Pierre to create a piece of custom artwork. It is a painting of me standing on top of the world happy with a smile and microphone, doing what I love to do. I talked to him so he was aware of the elements I needed represented. I made sure he presented everything as balanced and harmonious as I wanted to live my life. At the time I called on him, I was not quite in alignment with my mind-body-spirit-emotions-environment connection, but I wanted to see something every day that would encourage me to see my dream in full color and my soul as I wanted it to be. In this painting, I could be singing or speaking about my 5 Star Points system to others into this beautiful microphone that I always wanted, a specific model of jazz mic. I have other musicians behind me, planted and grounded in the earth with a strong foundation. This piece of art is filled with nods to the 5 Star Points and also features a rising sun and moon bringing light as I do what I know I want to do with my whole life, my life's purpose and what makes me want to get up each day. In this beautiful painting, I am filled to the brim with joy and peace. I hung it in the "fame and reputation" area I created so I could say, "This is me. This is who I am. My rays of light are mine, and I have manifested my dream and am living my life's purpose." Mind you, I was not there at all, but still, I had made the commitment that this was where I would go with the rest of my life. Now this painting is me, and I can share it with you so you know you can do it too if you take the action steps.

I did not even own that microphone when the painting was made, but the next Christmas, my brother purchased it for me. When I opened it up, I jumped for joy like the little girl who had wanted it so badly, had wanted nothing but to create and sing.

Later, this painting would inspire me on great days to keep going. Juiced up, I would continue writing, calling, organizing my finances. On days that were not so graceful, this painting would remind me of the purpose of all the hard work and that soon the 5 Star Points would click within me, and I would be fully in the glow of my own light.

I created more environmental affirmations to put all around me. We are constantly taking in environmental stimuli, whether we know it or not, that get absorbed into our beings. Environmental affirmations give you a reminder of the vision you have for your life. They get your mind and soul working on you, both consciously and subconsciously, when you see them.

Are You Distracted in Your Restful Environment?
There are some items that should never be in your room while you rest, because they distract you from finding peace and harmony so you can recharge and reconnect with your 5 Star Points foundation.

When I talked about the body, I explained that you need to get proper sleep in order to take care of your temple, and that means eliminating distractions like technology. I can make an exception for the parent who needs to keep his/her phone on when kids are out late with friends, but there is no reason to have your phone on by your bedside at night listening to every text or email as it comes in. We do not need to have our computer next to us, shining brightly, begging us to pick it up and take care of that one, last important email before we go to sleep. And we do not need to have our TVs on, as TVs are a distraction from sleep and rest. The principles of feng shui dictate that we should not have a TV in our bedroom at all. I enjoy television from time to time, but I am not the type with a million shows I need to keep up with. I enjoy relaxing in bed on a Sunday sometimes and watching good programs or movies, so even I have a TV in my room, but when I go to sleep, so does my television!

What about smart phones? People can get so lost in them! We are constantly checking our phones and playing with them, and as creative, we can lose so much valuable creating time through this practice. We become so glued to our phones that we feel empty without them at arm's reach. Look, I am a professional, independent entrepreneur who is all about being accessible. Being available for opportunities is how I have booked so many of my jobs. I have kept the phone by me, and when a client was trying to reach out to me before I had my executive assistant and manager, I was Johnny on the spot. I contacted them and made the booking go through before they could think about anyone else. But there came a point even then that I had to put my phone on silent. I had to be disciplined enough put it away when I was supposed to be busy creating. You can have your phone in your space; most of us have to these days. But you cannot allow yourself to get caught up in distracting phone calls. Set aside a special time when you can talk to you family or friends, but take your creative time seriously. Creating is essential to manifesting your dreams and fulfilling your life's purpose!

Make time and space to create and work towards your mission, purpose and intentions.

I have spoken to many creatives during my lifetime, and so many of them have talked about how they never have time to really get their work done. "Oh no?" I've asked. "I have no time" is just an excuse. Once we start to look at our lives, we find that we have plenty of time to devote to creative projects, or at least a few hours a day – enough time to make an impact. Even if you only have 30 minutes a day available, if you add that up over time you will actually have hours of time to devote in just one week. It may take you a little longer to complete your project, but you will have it in several months. Technology and other distractions can suck away our time before we know it!

I used to be big on the "I don't have time" excuse until I stopped and actually looked at where my time was going. Think about it: We have 24 hours in a day, 16 hours when we are not asleep. Even if we work an eight- hour shift somewhere then we still have eight hours left. Even when you take into account time spent cooking, eating, getting kids off to school, or whatever else is part of your daily routine, you still have time. Yes, you do! Most people do not work every single day, and many have the whole weekend off. Even if you can set aside 30 minutes a day to write work out, practice voice, draw, work on an invention, that's still 30 minutes of dedication! Even if you did this just four days a week, that would add up to two hours a week, which is six full hours of hard work each month. In three months, you will have 18 hours, and in six months, you will have 36 ... I think you see where this is going! You have no excuses not to create, even if you only have 30 minutes.

When I was searching for extra time, I used technology to see where my time was going and clocked every single thing I was doing each day. I discovered a truth through this process: We can get so caught up with what we are doing that we don't even know what we are doing. I used the clock program on my phone and had my assistant clock it in every time I did anything during the day. When I would take a break for TV, to surf the Internet, cook, work out, do homework or anything else, I would clock it.

Boy oh boy, did I have a rude awakening. I was surfing the Internet for way too long, casually looking at new fashions, shoes, fun videos of animals and other things unrelated to getting my music writing, CD or the seeds of this book squared away. I spent significant time on the computer doing tasks that were neither productive nor even necessary. At the end of the experiment, I found an extra two hours EVERY SINGLE DAY that were available for creation. I still do some fun surfing now, but I have minimized that a great deal. I save the fashion and animal video watching for when all my work is done for the day! I decided that while these activities bring me joy, they do not bring me enough joy to justify taking time away from continuing my life purpose and developing projects that will help me live my dream.

Make room for quiet time.

We need to have quiet time. When we are asleep is when we are the most vulnerable. Proper sleep is critical to keeping our bodies in alignment, and when there are too many distractions in the background, we are not really resting fully. Perhaps you fell asleep watching a positive, uplifting movie. But what if some intense horror movie comes on after that, or a news program depicting killing, molestation or some of the world's other horrors? You cannot protect yourself. You have no defense. You are asleep, and you are absorbing the negativity and bad news invading on your environment when you are supposed to be safe, resting and at peace. And then you wonder why you have nightmares or wake up feeling disturbed or disgruntled the next morning! When your sleeping environment is quiet, you will wake up feeling rested and at peace, ready to live out your dreams.

Feng Shui Crash Course

I could write a whole book just on Feng Shui ... and of course, many others have! But just so you can understand how my deep knowledge of this topic informs environment and the rest of the 5 Star Points, here is a little crash course.

In Feng Shui there are nine guas in the Bagua.

WEALTH & PROSPERITY purple, blues, reds	**FAME & REPUTATION** reds, oranges FIRE ELEMENT	**LOVE & MARRIAGE** pinks, reds, white
HEALTH & FAMILY greens, floral, stripes WOOD ELEMENT	**CENTER EARTH** yellows, earth tones EARTH ELEMENT	**CREATIVITY & CHILDREN** white, pastels METAL ELEMENT
KNOWLEDGE & SELF-CULTIVATION blues, green	**CAREER** black WATER ELEMENT	**HELPFUL PEOPLE & TRAVEL** grays, silver

The guas are as follows ...

★ Wealth and Prosperity

★ Fame and Repuation

★ Love and Marriage

★ Health and Family

★ Center

★ Creativity and Children

★ Knowledge and Self Cultivation

★ Career

★ Helpful People and Travel

If you look closely at these guas, you can really see that if you have all of these in order in your environment, you are living a pretty harmonious life. When I am doing a feng shui consultation, I am looking at all these elements and seeing how they can be strengthened so someone can live in a balanced, comfortable environment in their own place and be in alignment with their 5 Star Points.

Why is this harmony so important? You cannot create in a place that is not comfortable. You cannot create when you have clutter, or items that bring up negative memories from the past that you do not need to be thinking about.

As an example, I had a client that said she wanted two things: to start her design company; to welcome a new love into her life. This client was a fashion designer with a beautiful home, and to the naked eye, you would not think anything was wrong with her space. She was pretty neat and clean and she did not have a lot of work to do as far as over-all clutter, but she did indeed have issues within her inner environment that took her away from the two things she wanted most in her life.

She wanted to create a beautiful and romantic love affair that would turn into a beautiful marriage, but what I found in her seemingly beautiful home was that as much as she said this, she was not ready. Fortunately we were doing overall coaching where I was not only doing her home, but was also coaching her over time, and I saw items all over her home from her ex that she loved dearly. Simply put, she was not over him. She had his items in her home and all kinds of old memories, both good and bad, that were haunting her.

How could you make love to a new love with huge teddy bears and stuffed animals that were gifted to you by an ex-lover on the bed? Day in and day out, you would be blocked from your relationship evolving into something beautiful, because you would be looking at your ex-boyfriend and feeling his energy every night. This woman I consulted was literally sleeping with his energy right next to her and thus could not really move on, though the relationship had ended over a year earlier.

When I brought this to her attention, she could not believe it. She acknowledged she was unconsciously keeping him around and in her life. She insisted she was totally over him, but when I told her to dispose of his items and eliminate them from her environment, she did not want to. Later that night, she admitted her true feelings. The deeper we got into the session, the more she released. She knew that their relationship was not healthy, and that there was no reason for her to hold onto it so tightly. She finally consented to donate these items to charity and get them out of her environment. She needed her canvas clear in order to paint her new, joyful picture! She needed to break up with her story in order to create her dream life. She needed to make her home into a place that was a beautiful extension of her.

While going through this client's home, I also discovered she had the messiest, most disorganized office I had ever seen. It shocked me, since she was so neat, clean and organized otherwise that she had all her food broken down into categories and labeled in the freezer. How could her office, the place where she created, be in such disarray? She admitted her creativity felt stifled, and I was not surprised! This room was the creative center of her home, and it gave her no space to create. There was more memorabilia from her old relationship, no designated workspace to design, and a non-working printer. She had no technology that would help her do anything she needed to advance her business or her life. And let me tell you, when I called it to her attention, excuse after excuse filled the air, and I could tell she was living with these same excuses day after day. Her daily routine was "start and stop," and I could see why: Her creative space was full of dysfunctional items, disappointments and distractions. Her home office was set up for failure rather than productivity and success. How could she ever get into a flow? We all must set up our environment for success, comfort and an energy that will allow us to focus and create with grace and ease.

Overall there were minor fixes to be made around her home, but the issues she was having in her internal environment were clearly showing up in her external environment. This story illustrates why the 5 Star Points is so special: You can see by revisiting this woman's space with me just how interrelated mind, body, spirit, emotions and environment are. You cannot have a strong foundation unless you have all the 5 Star Points in alignment.

This woman focused on two sore spots in her home and was forced to look inside herself. This experience is exactly why I went to get certified in feng shui, because it was the moment I finally understood how the home was a reflection of what was going on inside the homeowner. This client had to go inside and find out why she was keeping negative energy and energy from her past relationship around. She had to face the facts, figure out why she was holding on for dear life to unproductive things, come to terms with that reason and find peace in the situation for the betterment of herself and so she could live out her life's purpose unhindered.

Take Back the Power in Your Environment and in Your Soul

When this beautiful ray of light / creator faced her fears with me she was able to take back her power. She was able to stand in her light and rejoice. She made a choice and made her declaration that night. She set her intention, and we worked on affirmations that would support her on a daily basis outside our coaching sessions. We devised a plan for those rooms to be handled so that she could get a handle on her career, her life's purpose and her dream. She identified the mission and purpose behind her designs and determined that what made her excited was that she was giving back to this world, and this gave her strength. She cried tears of joy, and I knew they were real. Being a designer was not a get-rich-quick scheme, but something real in her heart. When you find that fire and have the rest of the 5 Star Points in place, there is nothing that can stop you!

She moved forward with cleaning, organizing and energizing her space, and shortly thereafter, I was celebrating with her! Her line was flourishing, and so was her love life. She found the type of man that she could not believe was possible to have in her life. Her past abusive relationships were a thing of the past.

She filled her office, the knowledge and self-cultivation center of her bagua with lots of items that supported the manifestation of her dream: vision boards; a mission and purpose statement and all kinds of positive reinforcement with lots of self-love, self-honor and self-respect. She fell in love with herself and loved herself so much that she started to shine brightly. She even stood differently and acted differently. There was no more moping! She walked around with confidence, and attracted someone who loved himself and was a truly great man. And guess what? I was not surprised by her success!

The environment of our home goes right back inside us. I worked through her environment, and it pointed right back to the 5 Star Points of how she thought and how she treated herself. She was able to reconnect to her spirit and use her emotions to tap right back into her fears so she could confront them and be self-loving. From one point to the next, she got back to the core and was able to shine like the star that she was. And you can do it too! When you change your energy like she did, it reverberates so strongly that your spirit cannot help but reverberate, and your light will shine, shine, shine from the center of you!

Get your chi a-flowing!

Your chi is your life energy, and you need to get it flowing. A happy, healthy environment leads to a happy, healthy mind, body and spirit. When your environment is full of positive energy you will feel balanced and harmonious, be able to create with grace and ease and be free of distractions so you can focus on working diligently and playing with comfort and energy.

Your home must make you feel protected so your nervous system can relax. There are so many dangers in the world, and at home, you need to feel protected. Your outer reality, which includes your home, is a snapshot of what is going on inside you. This home can be a lovely space that others can experience as an extension of your authentic self. When you feel comfortable identifying with your place as an expression of you feeling proud and at ease, you will be able to create a safe haven in which to play, create, relax and have others over to celebrate life.

To create a real flow in your home, take pride in your space, no matter how small it is. If you cannot take care of even the smallest space, how can you take care of a medium space, a large space ... or yourself? Taking care of your environment and yourself shows you are grateful for your life and all the time and space you have on this earth. And that creates space to welcome in the bigger and better opportunities that will come when you are focused on manifesting your dreams and living your life's purpose.

Create an Environment for *You*

When you are reprogramming your environment, you must create a space full of joy and your intentions. Do not look at changing your environment as work; look at it as accessing joy! Most importantly, create a space that is all about self-honor and self-love. Do not let others' opinions influence what you put in your home to support yourself. Instead, think about what you need to have around you in order to manifest your dreams, honors you and celebrates what you enjoy!

Environment Exercise #1: Distraction Elimination List

What is distracting you, bothering you and disturbing your peace?

★ *Create a list of distractions in your environment and make a plan to cut them out!*

Yes! I encourage you to create a list of distractions in your environment and your life to see what is zapping your energy and blocking you from fully manifesting your dreams and living your life's purpose. What is getting in your way?

Here is a sample list. (Please make your own!)

★ My "day job"
★ Arguments I have with my wife/husband/mom/daughter/son
★ The mess in my house
★ Health issues I have not addressed
★ Lack of money

Many times we have to look at what is distracting us in order to clear our space to make room for what we want. Now, make a list of distractions, and start working to take action to clear them up so you can make more space in your environment for YOU to thrive!

Environment Exercise #2: Feng Shui of the Soul

When you are not sure where to begin cleaning up and rearranging your environment for better flow, or are not sure if you are on the right track towards creating positive forces in your life, visualize! Every time you are thinking about bringing something new into your space ...

★ *Visualize how something you want feels in your space with you, in your home, around you and see if it really resonates. Think about how it contributes to your mind-body-spirit-emotions-environment connection, what it is worth to you personally and exactly what you are willing to do to have it.*

Can you imagine it? Does it make you happy? Write down your feelings about it, then bring it on in!

It is easy to make up all the excuses in the world about why we do not have what we want, need or love. But it is within our power to let go of everything that is blocking us from feeding our soul. We need to stop working ourselves up into a frenzy, riding the emotional roller coaster and constantly asking, "Should I?" Look within yourself and change your environment!

Environment Exercise #3: Make Room in Your Soul
This one's a biggie!

> ★ *Make room in your soul for whatever it is you love.*

Now that we've been through all the 5 Star Points together, and you've been doing some exercises, it is time for me to ask you to do something huge: Make some room in your soul for your dream. If you have read this whole book so far and avoided saying your dream out loud, now is the time to identify it. Call it by name! Then decide it is your priority and that you are going to make it come true. You can absolutely make the time to allow your dream to manifest and to clear out what is holding you back so you have the space to call in something beautiful.

When you wholeheartedly grab your dream – whether it is a supportive partner, a fulfilling project or something else – you need to make way for the loving energy that will enhance your internal and external space and help you move forward. This is feng shui of the soul, and the key to transforming your environment!

Nurturing your Environment: Accountability Chart
Use this chart to track the progress you make creating a peaceful relationship with your ENVIRONMENT each month. Put self-nurturing activities you engage in that help you create a peaceful environment that reflects your authentic self on the left-hand side, and every day you focus on the activities listed, give yourself a check mark!

ACCOUNTABILITY CHART

I am nurturing my environment this month by...

Example: Addressing the distraction of X in my life and clearing it out so I can make more room for my creative work

	M	T	W	Th	F	S	Su	M	T	W	Th	F	S	Su	M	T	W	Th	F	S	Su	M	T	W	Th	F	S	Su

CHAPTER 7

Revamping Your Money Mindset

"Wealth consists not in having great possessions, but in having few wants." **– Epictetus**

Money, money, money! What would we do without money? We need it, we want it ... we think about it, we work for it ... we love it and we hate it. We can enjoy life with it, or we can agonize over it. Money can help us achieve our goals, or it can deplete us and prevent our dreams from coming true. Money can take us up the right road, or down the wrong path. We can be smart about money, or we can be ignorant about it.

Do you know what money even does for us – what its purpose is? There is nothing else in life that is both more important and more insignificant than money. When I discuss money with others, they usually get all worked up. They get weird and closed off ... or they get excited, and their unrealistic expectations about how money contributes to their lives come exploding out.

I used to have what I thought was a bad relationship with money. As I thought about really focusing on my artistry, I agonized over how I would pay my bills. I had to focus, but all I could think about was how I would maintain my lifestyle and how I could make money come to me.

I spent so much time agonizing over dark thoughts about money that I paralyzed myself from moving forward. Sure I had some good reasons why it was not the best time to put my CD out, for example, but some of what I was telling myself – a lot of it in fact – was just excuses.

I know this now, because once I actually decided to move forward with my album on my birthday, it was just nine months later that I released *Spirit of Oya*. I took my dream from start to finish, everything included, from fantasy, to real world in just nine months.

Instead of filling your head with thoughts of "I can't," agonizing over the money and letting that money paralyze you from moving forward, I encourage you to focus on how you can make your dreams happen using money as a tool to move forward.

You need money.

Was that statement hard for you to read? Did that bring up all kinds of fears, anxieties, negative thoughts, chaotic emotions? Did that make your spirit and your soul feel heavy? Well, it's true! You do need money. If you do not believe me, let's take a closer look at what money really means, and how it can help positively contribute to manifesting your dreams and living your life's purpose. We all need to understand how we relate to money – how we work with it, earn it, spend it, lose it, invest it and ask for it – in order to make it work as a positive force in our lives.

A Brief History of Money

Money gets us what we want. It is a medium of exchange, and a piece of paper that facilitates trade.

Before there was money, there was barter. People exchanged things of value for other things of value they needed. They exchanged what they had for what they wanted and granted the person that had what they wanted something the other person needed. The exchange was mutually beneficial. Everyone was happy!

Later, coins came into play. The coins were made of precious metals that people could attribute a set value to. They were made of silver or gold, and because people knew these metals were precious, they knew the coins had real value that could be exchanged for the things they wanted and needed.

Much later, paper money came into play. I know how very convenient paper money is, but I can also see how, especially back then but also now, people could get confused by the actual worth of a piece of paper. That piece of paper gets its worth based on the worth we assign to it. We say it is worth $1, $5, $10, $20, $50,$100, and so forth, and it is. It is based on the original theory behind coins made of precious metals, but most people do not see it that way.

You might be wondering, "Why is she talking about the history of money? How does this help me manifest my dreams?" I am talking about this because I want you to see the value of money in a different way. I want you to disconnect the value of money from your fears about making, keeping and having money and understand how money actually relates directly to your self-worth.

What are You Worth?

Someone taught me a long time ago that time is money and money is time. How much do you want for your time? What are you worth?

On a practical level, what you are worth is all about setting rates. And setting your rates means taking into account your cost of living, what you want to save, what you have invested and the going rate in the marketplace – what others at your level of experience get paid to do what you do.

Also, the way I see it, my precious time is like a precious metal. If you are going to hire me, you need to give me what my time is worth in the form of money, and this concept is actually not that much different from the barter system.

Still, people get so very strange when the topic of money comes up. Many find asking for it difficult, and this causes them to set their rates too low or to let people take advantage of them.

What is your time worth to others?

When you are setting your rates, you do need to take into account what others are willing and able to pay for your gifts and services. What is what you do worth to other people? What value does it add to their lives? What would you honestly pay for your own services if you were looking for what you offer? Would you want to cut deals, or would you be able to see the inherent value and be willing to pay yourself your service price?

On the one hand, if you would not pay your service price and the rate you are charging, then why would you expect someone else to pay it?

On the other hand, what you do is worth something; your talents, time and life's purpose – the thing you are great at – are really worth something. The question is, how much? And who should you be marketing to in order to connect with others who see the value in what you do who will happily hand over the dough for your expertise?

What are you worth to YOU?

How much are you worth? That can be a tough question for many of us to ask ourselves, but valuing yourself inside, and aligning that self-worth with the actions you take in your life are very important to honoring your spirit and letting your light shine bright.

With that idea in mind, dig a little deeper: Do you think what you do in your life is important? Do you feel that what you charge for the work you do is enough? Are you happy every time you get money from your client, or do you find yourself experiencing guilt or resentment?

In other words, are the actions you take aligning with what you are truly worth on the inside?

I want to share my own personal experiences and feelings about self-worth with you. When I am on stage, I like to know that I am valued – that I am getting what I am worth. When you are a musician, there is nothing more frustrating than getting ready for a show, miserably putting on your clothes and packing up because you know you are giving more than you are getting – that you are giving more of yourself and putting more time and energy into a gig or project than it is really worth.

Have you ever felt like that? You don't even have to be a performer to understand the feeling of doing a job and absolutely hating it. We have already talked about that negative feeling many times in this book. You might have felt annoyed, and you may have even snapped at people for no reason, when it wasn't their fault that you took the gig. The truth is, if you have found yourself in that frustrating situation, you have to realize, YOU and only YOU made the decision to get involved. It wasn't the client's or anyone else's fault that you were there.

You might be thinking, "But I need the money." Sure, we all "need" the money. (And I realize that sometimes we all have had to do what we "need" to do, whether to prevent ourselves from getting kicked out of our homes, or because our kids need to eat.) But what about those times when you do not "need" it? Why are you selling yourself short?

None of us like the desperate feeling of doing work for less than we are worth because we "need" the money. So, in those times when you do not "need" it, think about what you would expect if you could "really use the money"; don't do work for less just because you are desperate for the cash ... no matter what! If you do, you are setting yourself up to be undervalued.

Why would you let people think you are worth less when you know you should be getting paid more? That is a dangerous message to send out to the masses, and it will ensure people continuously call you back to do them a $50 favor, whether those people are potential clients, friends or anyone else.

The answer is to be secure with your rates. When you tell someone how much you charge, you have to say it with confidence. Be firm. Be confident. When you stutter or act uncomfortable, you are sending a message that you are unsure of your own worth. And if you are working these 5 Star Points every day and truly living your life's purpose, you know you are priceless!

Of course, sometimes it is important for all of us to be flexible. And I love what I do, but I am not going to allow a client to talk me down to a "deal" that is not right for myself and for my musicians. And I would not go to a client's workplace and ask that client to work for $5 an hour when they are supposed to be making much more than that for their expertise.

A music teacher once told me that he tells his students to charge people for all the years they put into school and learning to be who they are, just like anyone else. And that makes total sense! Whether you spent time and energy on school, or on developing your talent and experience, you need to charge for all those years you put into the work you do.

Believe in your worth ... and let that show in everything you do and are!

You are worth way, way more than the money you receive for what you do.

When I stand at my booth after a show and tell people the cost of my *Spirit of Oya* CD, I stand tall and proud, happily giving a price without stuttering or budging. I thought about the price for a long time and really educated myself. I looked up how much it cost to produce the product, compared going rates against the value and confidently set my price. If someone says something like, "That seems like a lot of money," or "How can you get away with charging that much?" I am not moved, because I did my homework. If they do not want to buy it, fine! I know its worth, and I'm sticking to it!

... Enough already with the "starving artist" bit!

As creatives, many of us are stuck in the artist with poverty mentality, because that is what we learned, whether from society, our parents, or some other authority figure who had an effect on our lives and thought he/she could dictate how we felt about ourselves and our dreams and how we should be living. These naysayers told us artists always struggle. That is just the way it is, because people just do not pay for good art.

Unfortunately, there will probably always be people out there who believe that if you choose an artist's life, you are just playing around. These people believe being an artist is not a "serious" job like a doctor, lawyer or someone else who "deserves" to be paid well for his/her work: "You will never be able to make a living! How will you support your family?" There are so many hang-ups out there just oozing out of other people that it perpetuates our poverty mentality and pulls us from our guitars, microphones, paint brushes, pens and papers. When the going gets really tough, some of us might even give up and leave for what we perceive is a more "dependable" or stable job that just leaves us miserable, because it does not fulfill our life's purpose.

Believe in your worth!

If you do not believe in yourself, then who will believe in you? If you are iffy about your rate, then people will be iffy about paying what you say you deserve. If you do not confidently disclose your rates when asked, then you are communicating that you question your own worth or that you do not know how to talk about money gracefully. That energy gets sent out to a potential client, and that client will question everything about you.

You must be able to talk about what you do and how much you deserve to be compensated for it in a clear, concise and confident way. If you are worried you cannot do this, just remember the "3 Cs":

★ Clear
★ Concise
★ Confident

If you can remember those, no one will ever be able to question you again. They will know you mean business: This is what you charge, and if they cannot pay it or are unwilling to pay it, they have to move on.

We have been told for so long that we are not worth the money we want that we block our own thoughts and do not attract those that will pay us properly.

Confession time: I used to have a major issue about money and determining what to charge. I did not want to lose the job, so I would negotiate, and then I would not always feel joyful while doing the actual job, because I would know I had way undercharged. It would make me feel worthless.

Have you been to this negative place? You get on the job and you realize how much work it actually is, how much extra money you have to spend on new clothes, rehearsing, memorizing, creating, refining, hair, makeup, nails. You realize you forgot how much actually goes into the rate you charge, and you end up actually losing money on a job.

Take "Service" Jobs Sparingly ... and Do Them from Your Heart

I had a client ask me recently to produce a project, and when I did the math, I realized that after flying out to the city she was in to do the job and paying for all the things that went into the job, I was not going to make my worth. I was not going to be paid appropriately for the work and the skill set I was offering her.

While the work you do is not always about the money, money does play a part in everything you do. If you see that you will get something out of doing a job that has a value beyond money, you can certainly barter. But if you are going to do these "service" jobs for friends and co-creators, you have to make sure you are getting something precious in return. If what you are getting cannot be measured in dollars, make sure there is real value attached, whether it be free publicity that lead to increased sales of your services and products or something else good. Giving away your divine energy for free does not make sense and is not healthy for you! It does not contribute to strengthening the foundation rooted in your 5 Star Points, nor does it help you manifest your dreams and live your life's purpose.

It can be a fantastic experience to do service jobs. I do them! But you must make sure you are doing them for the right reasons. Are you doing them from your heart in order to enrich your community and help others? That is beautiful! But sometimes people will use your sense of philanthropy to get an artist to do something and tug at their heartstrings. These people will try to get something for free without the best of intentions. This is why you must be very careful about where and when and to what you donate your time.

Charging for Your Services

Just like a doctor or a lawyer, you put in time and energy to be the best you, and don't you forget that! For some this is a revolutionary concept, but we have to get over ourselves and charge appropriate rates!

I have included this chapter about money in this book so you understand it, because money is essential to understanding your self-worth ... which is essential to understanding your connection to the 5 Star Points.

What is the value of you, and what do people see in you?

Change your thought patterns surrounding self-worth and how you see money.

You have to figure out what your minimum fee is. As model Linda Evangelista notoriously said, "We don't wake up for less than $10,000 a day." What amount will you wake up for? How much do you need to be paid to walk out the door, travel to your destination and get your spirit to really show up and shine?

Your rate needs to be well thought-out.

Know your hourly rate, your project rate and what you are willing to negotiate down to and up to respectively and happily. Most importantly, never let anyone see you sweat or hear you stuttering! This means you cannot think about what you want to charge on the fly. Think about it carefully on your own before you show up to negotiate (or not negotiate!), so when you have the conversation, you are secure and can present reasons why your rate is what it is. Period.

I have had prospective clients say to me, "Well, the 'Joe Blow Band' is willing to charge $400 for a trio and vocalist for three sets."

Well, there is a reason someone is calling YOU. If they really want you, they will pay your value. You are not the "Joe Blow Band." I personally know any trio I am involved in is worth more than $400, and if that band is willing to do it for that price for whatever reason, I let them! If the prospective client wants to go with that band, I cannot control it. But I am not going to underbid them when I know that is not my rate. My musicians work with the top music artists in the music industry. I am honored to be working with them, and I am clearly not going to be paying them $50 - $100.

We all start somewhere.

We all start somewhere, and sometimes you have to start your rates lower than is ideal in order to get yourself established and gain experience. Become polished and professional, but after you pay your dues, please, please, PLEASE adjust your rates and be comfortable with your decision to do that! I made "Joe Blow Band"-equivalent rates when I was in elementary school and junior high doing fashion shows and sing-ing, so clearly after all these years, I have earned the right to charge more, and I must pay my co-creators appropriately.

Never stink of desperation!

We all need to eat. (Revisit the chapter on Body if you don't believe me!) And I respect any artist that will negotiate and take certain jobs sometimes when they really, really, REALLY need the money. But do not, I repeat, DO NOT make this a habit. You do not want the whole world to know that an artist well worth $1,000 worked for $100. How do you explain to the man that paid you $1,000 that you did the same show for $100 for another client? You just can't. Not only is that situation unfair to the client that paid more, but it is unfair to you!

Stop living in fear about money!

In order to develop a healthy attitude about money, you have to stop being scared. Who are you and what is your worth? Once you know this for certain, you can approach any client with total confidence with your rates. The worst that can happen is the client will say, "No." And, of course, you need to be ready for that scenario. But when you put your foot down and tell a client your proper rate, you must also be ready for the client to say YES with ease!

Sometimes a client will call me and just not have enough money to cover my expenses, let alone to pay for me and my band, and that is just not a good fit. Again, we earned it, and I have been doing this long enough to feel comfortable living with this concept.

You may still feel weird about money. A lot of people feel strange dis-cussing their own worth and value, and that is why we cannot jump ahead and just gloss over the 5 Star Points. We have to really work them and establish a strong mind-body-spirit-emotions-environment connec-tion so our foundation inside is strong enough for us to do the math and feel comfortable discussing our rates.

Self-management skills and a sales pitch can help prevent desperation.

If you are going to be any type of artist, you will likely have a period of time when you are just starting out when you cannot afford management or an assistant. You must learn how to manage yourself, your money and your work without the help of others. People can sniff out self-doubt very easily, so before you get on sales calls with people, practice out loud in the room with friends or fellow musicians. Get that sales pitch down!

Some prospective clients ask me to explain my rates. They do not mean any harm or any disrespect; they just do not understand how I work and how I set my rates, and they just want it explained to them. We have to be a little forgiving of those that are not enmeshed in the Arts; they do not understand how the system works or how we assign value.

When I take the time to explain, some clients are not interested. Others say, "Wow! I had no idea all that is involved in this. Let me work out the budget." And others understand completely and put the money in my account in a flash.

Be prepared to stand up for yourself just as your manager would if you had one and explain your rates respectfully and professionally. Perhaps you feel that this practice will make others think you are cocky. First of all, remember that your life is first and foremost about YOU and manifesting YOUR dreams; worrying about what others think of you is just a distraction from letting your authentic spirit shine. Be confident in yourself and your fellow co-creators. Know you are worth it, and that your work speaks for itself!

Put Yourself before Your Money Hang-ups
When any of us really, really want something, we will pay for it. When you want a beautiful, high-quality designer dress or suit or want to take a fabulous vacation, you will pay what it costs. You pay because you want the best experience, not just something mediocre, something that will "do" for now. So, why would you put a lower value than top dollar on your beautiful talents, on your spirit and on the experience of all of you?

What we put out there is what we get back. If you put out high-level professional services, you will get people that respect your expertise and want to pay for those services. Maybe you are not convinced right off that bat. That's OK! Everyone is different. Some of us need to move towards believing in our worth in steps.

Take me, for instance: I have always known I had talent, but I did wonder if I could turn my dreams into a lifelong adventure and be prosperous. I had to go through some calculated steps to get to a place where I fully believed in my ability to manifest my dreams and live my life's purpose. I proved to myself that what I was doing made sense. I tried it out, making small investments in advertising my services, and I would instantly get a return. When I would make the money back plus more, that proved to me what I was doing was working.

Set your intention and follow through with action steps.
I did not truly start to come into my own mind-body-spirit-emotions-environment connection until I set my intention and started taking action steps to achieve my goals. The day I sang at my grandmother's funeral changed my life and understanding of who I am as an artist and entrepreneur, what I represent and why I do what I do. As I was singing, I was reminded of the three-year old me that sang in church with my father, and the little five-, six- and seven-year old girl playing initially nonsensical chords on my aunt's piano, singing about roller skating.

What was the common thread? In all these instances, I was bringing joy to people's hearts, whether these people were family members, members of my church congregation or those attending one of my gigs. They smiled with me. They sang. They danced and clapped. I was having a ball, I was stirring up emotions, I was living my dream, and I knew there was great value in what I was bringing to others. Just as I will pay handsomely to see my favorite artist, I expect that those who want to receive my spirit will pay to see me sing my heart out.

Once I realized how valuable my talent is, I started to really have fun. I started to see how I can make others feel deep emotions, release tension and stress, be encouraged, inspired and energized. That is really worth something! Isn't it?

You must see yourself as worth something great in order to get something great.

"I AM a Success"

I make this statement when I speak to groups about the 5 Star Points system. It shocks people sometimes, because they are terrified to say it themselves. At first, I was reluctant to say it, because I did not want to brag or seem like an arrogant diva, especially when in the company of others who were not doing quite so well, or those who felt very weighed down because they were disconnected from their authentic selves and their heartfelt dreams and were unable to see a way out.

When other musicians would say, "It's really hard out here," I would secretly think, "Not really." But I didn't think I could say that. How DARE I? Again, it is how you think that is at the root of this, and that is why I want you to really say your "I am"s and work through the 5 Star Points system very consciously, with your whole mind and your whole self.

When you get out of the mindset of "It's hard out here, and I can't make any real money," you will see that anything is possible, and positive energy will flow to you. You will manifest your dreams and live your life's purpose. It may sound simple, but that is because it is! The challenge is getting out of the self-doubt and negative self-talk that keeps holding you back, keeps you from earning what you are worth and then some.

When I came into my own after doing so much work through my own system, I finally was able to stand up for myself – my whole self!

- ★ I AM A BRIGHT LIGHT.
- ★ I AM WONDERFUL.
- ★ I AM AWESOME.
- ★ I AM WORTHY.
- ★ I AM PROSPERING AND SHARING MY TALENTS WITH THE WORLD.

Once I connected to these positive, activating thoughts in my heart, my spirit and soul, I made up my mind that there was no stopping. I set my rates, enjoyed the work and believed in myself and my dream!

Be the Best!

If you want top dollar, you need to find yourself doing top things! You must practice to be the best, be organized and professional. Clients have a lot of options, so if you can confidently go out there and be the best, people will pay for it.

I hear a lot of creatives complain they are not earning what they deserve, but then I look and see they are not actually doing what they need to do to be the best. They neither look nor speak the part.

I am a firm believer in the "no excuses" motto. I have certainly made excuses in my life, but I understand that is no way to manifest your dreams and live your life's purpose. There can be zero excuses when you really want to succeed. If you say "never," it will never happen.

You must make your own dreams happen. You must sit down and write out all your options – because you have options! There are steps you can take to reach your goal with grace, and there is no such thing as "no way," because, as they say, "where there is a will, there is a way!"

You will do whatever it takes to be the best, just as I am up right now until the wee hours writing this chapter so I can complete this book and share it with you. I have been wanting to complete this book for a very long time, and when it hit me that NOW was the time, I made the commitment, and here I am to follow through. You will know when YOUR time comes, and it is your choice to answer the door to your dreams.

Do Not Let Money Be an Excuse

Do not let money or your fear of money be an excuse not to move forward! Be smart, and make smart choices. You do not have to quit your job and go "all in," setting yourself up for failure if you do not have a plan or a cushion (and in fact, you absolutely shouldn't). Support yourself through the job you have, and give thanks for that job, or find a job that can support you and gives you some free hours to work on your dream, and over time, it will happen.

It is possible to live off an artist's income.

We just have to be smart about how we earn our money, use it and save it. Trust me, you can make money being creative. The question is how you work with the money you make, and how you put it towards continuing to do exactly what you came here to do: Live your dream!

Money Exercise #1: "If I won the lotto, I would ..."
Quick! Without thinking, consider this question:

> ★ *If you won $10 million in the lottery right now, what would you do?*

Write down your gut response. Do not read ahead!

> ★ *Now, make a longer list of the little things in your life you would take care of if you suddenly had $10 million at your disposal.*

As an example, here is my list!

1. I would pay off all my debt.
2. I would get a financial advisor to put my money in proper places so I could live off it.
3. I would buy a beautiful home and create a fabulous living and creative space.
4. I would take care of my mom and brother.
5. I would create and work on my projects with gusto.
6. I would complete my projects.
7. I would continue with my music and film projects and seek out new opportunities in the Arts.

What did you come up with? There is no wrong answer! For many, this clears up a lot of issues within all the elements of their 5 Star Points, because it forces them to think about their lives from a heart-centered space. Some people might say, "I would never work again!" But if your heart is truly centered on creating, you will create even when money is not an object. You will do it because it is nestled deep within your heart and spirit.

Money Exercise #2: Providing for Your Needs
Knowing how much money you need to live and thrive is one way you can get over your fear of money for good! When you know how much

money you need, bottom line, to take care of your needs, you will be better equipped to make a plan rooted in the 5 Star Points that will help you achieve your goals.

★ *Make a budget for your dream life.*

I want you to make a budget for your dream life. Not a budget that will just allow you to "get by," but a budget that will allow you to enjoy your life and take the steps towards manifesting your dreams. Start with the basics like rent, food, clothing and transportation ... but then, please think bigger! If you need to keep a "day job," how much money will you need to give yourself the time and space to create and start laying a foundation for building your dreams? And how much will you need to give yourself time off to recharge, time for those massages and treats for your body, mind and spirit?

Write it down.

Money Exercise #3: Building a Bridge to Success

When I was first building a life rooted in the 5 Star Points, I needed to reprogram myself in steps so I could formulate action items that would help me manifest my dreams and live my life's purpose. You too can build a bridge to success, so you can be and do everything you ever dreamed and shine your light far and wide.

★ *Make a clear list of steps you will need to take in order to achieve your heartfelt dream.*

What are some steps you will need to take to get from point A (where you are now), to Point B (where you want to be, fully connected to your mind, body, spirit, emotions and environment, living the life you always wanted for yourself)? You may not be able to identify them all right now, because you may still be confused about how you can possibly make your dreams come true ... and that is OK! Write down what you can, set it aside, keep working on the 5 Star Points, and come back to it regularly to revise. You can and will get to the finish line!

CONCLUSION: Go Forth, and Manifest Your Dreams to Live Your Life's Purpose!

Now that have read this book, it is time for you to be with yourself, with your mind, body, spirit, emotions and in your environment and honor your own belief in yourself and your dreams. You were put on this earth to share your talents, and though people will have opinions about who you are and what you are doing with your life, you need to know that this is *your* life to do with it as you choose. Bask in your power of choice, and take the action steps needed to live your life's purpose!

We Are Creators and Co-Creators

We are brilliant creators, creating all the time. We are also co-creators, channeling God and working alongside our spirits to support our own dreams and spread our lights, encouraging others to do the same. I believe that if we work with our spirit and the talents that have been given to us by a higher power, we can channel God and co-create some of the most amazing work, beyond the current conscious limits of our imagination. We are spiritual beings having a human experience, co-creating with God, our spirit source and letting that energy swirl into a powerful and divine creation.

Our industry can be a tough one.

The creative industry will eat you up and spit you out if you let it. As I mentioned before, there are not many artists who can handle the business side of their careers, nor are there many who can afford to hire professional help to handle it for them right off the bat. Learn all you can about the business side of your career and be self-sufficient and self-loving. Keep your eye on the prize of building a foundation firmly planted in the 5 Star Points that will allow you to build that bridge towards manifesting your dreams and living your life's purpose, brick by brick.

Your Leap of Faith

Let's go back to the mind for a minute. How we think – about every-thing – is so important. Every thought we think, every word we say and every action step we take gives the universe a message about exactly what we want to manifest. But sometimes we need to push the limits of what our mind can envision and take a leap of faith, or better yet, build that bridge across the chasm between where we are now and living our life's purpose, fueled by our dreams.

When you take that leap of faith, it will feel like a risk. It might be scary. But if you know that God has your back, you love yourself, believe in yourself and have a solid action plan, your mind will hop on board and help you build your bridge across the chasm of fear and doubt and lead you into your new life spent manifesting your dreams and living your life's purpose. The real leap of faith is setting your intention to go towards your authentic, joyful self and sticking to it!

Commit, Commit, Commit!

In order to unlock the key to your authentic self and create a life firmly planted in the principles of the 5 Star Points system, you must commit. You must commit to your authentic self, in all its gorgeous glory. I know honoring your authentic self is not always easy, especially when you have so many competing energies pulling you here, there and everywhere, but you must commit. Make a commitment to saying "I am me," and to participating in heartfelt actions that show love to yourself and gratitude for this journey we are all on together.

Parting Gifts

Before we part ways for now, I have some final questions to ask you about what you have just read – about manifesting your own dreams and living your life's purpose.

- ★ Do you want to get a deeper sense of who you really are, from the top of your head to the tips of your toes?
- ★ Are you actually looking for opportunities?
- ★ Are you making yourself and your whole spirit available?
- ★ Are people aware of you and your gifts?
- ★ Do you want to let people love you, support you and spread your good news as you turn on your bright light for the whole world to see?
- ★ Then what are you waiting for?

Take the steps towards success and fulfillment!

What are you doing every day, every week and every month to keep your feet moving forward on the road towards manifesting your dreams? First of all, if you are on the road and already trucking along, congratulations! You have already succeeded.

Now, what are you doing to take you to the places you want to go? You have to stay on top of your game, fully alive and aware of your mind, spirit, body, emotions and environment, or you will get detoured or stuck standing in place on your very special path.

If you feel stuck, what is holding you back? What is blocking you from your dream? What about yourself are you judging?

Accentuate the Positive!

I've said it several times now, but I encourage you – no, I IMPLORE you – as you move towards getting everything you ever dreamed of in your life (and then some!) please keep a positive focus on yourself and your purpose. Stop saying, "I can't" and "I am unable to."

Affirm yourself with "I am!" Be sure of yourself, even when you are not completely sure what you want yet. In time, these positive vibes and glowing energy change you and the energy around you, and you will shift.

Revolutionize Your Life

When you have dealt with a set of circumstances for a long time, you will no longer see that they can be changed. If you feel stuck and tired, you do not have to stay stuck and tired! You might be used to that way of being, but you can change. Think of your soul as a computer. It has been running the same, outdated program for so long that it does not know how to do anything else. It is your responsibility to write a new program, so you can keep your computer running efficiently. This process will take time, but eventually, you will reboot and see the new path to manifesting your dreams, brimming with limitless possibilities!

Change your story NOW.

If you are afraid to change your story, get out of the past and move into the future, just remember: Everyone will hear your new story according to their own level of consciousness, and that is not your problem! Some will say your work is amazing, while others will say it is not so great. You have to do what is the very best for YOU and you alone, so you can love you and love your life, and so no matter what happens or what others say, you are comfortable, at peace and happy.

How is your Mind-Body-Spirit-Emotions-Environment connection NOW?
Let's revisit the exercise we did at the very beginning of this book and check in with ourselves.

Now that you have pages upon pages of proof of the inextricable link between your MIND, BODY, SPIRIT, EMOTIONS, and ENVIRONMENT ...

> ★ **On a scale of 1 to 5 (with 5 being the highest), how would you rate your mind-body-spirit-emotions-environment connection?**

Is your **MIND** still empowering you, or is it regularly saying, "I can't," "I won't," or "I'll never"?

Are you keeping your **BODY** feeling good and like a well-oiled machine that carries you through your days, or are you still perpetuating unhealthy habits like excessive drinking, smoking, and not eating properly?

Does your **SPIRIT** feel full of intuition, love, radiance, and creativity that allows you to prosper, or does it still feel a little tired, broken and in need of a tune-up?

Are your **EMOTIONS** in check and making you feel fully connected to the excitement of life, or are they still overwhelming you, weighing you down, and creating a tornado inside you?

Is your **ENVIRONMENT** pristine, comfortable, bright, and fueling your creative efforts, or is it still a cluttered, negative space, full of heavy darkness?

How do you rate? Write it down, and compare it to your original answers. Are you surprised by the difference?

Timing is Everything

Life is all about timing. You have to be truly ready to strengthen your mind-body-spirit-emotions-environment connection if you want to get going on manifesting your dreams and living your life's purpose. You can talk about it all you want, but until you are truly ready, and your blood is boiling ... and your heart is pounding ... and the energy is really inside you, moving you to take action, you will not be ready to make magic happen.

The universe will be ready when you are! When you make the decision to manifest your dreams, it will meet you halfway there, if not more. I have found this to be true every time I have made the decision to start projects that supported me on every level. When I finally made the choice to create my CD, miracles began to happen. People I needed showed up and helped me get to the finish line.

As much as I believe in spirit and that God has my back, there is really an awesome power in deciding and choosing to move forward. Once you get going with manifesting your dream and are serious about it, opportunities will come and take you to the next level, bringing your dream into real-world reality.

Picture This

Picture yourself sitting outside. It's a warm day, and the sun shines brightly down on you. You feel the rays. You feel the heat. The energy moves through you. It gives you a feeling of being alive, of life itself. Light is life. Not unlike the sun, we all have a light, a unique ray of light that MUST be shared. We all have a purpose.

For the world to illuminate, each ray of light must be present, each ray must shine. We all have gifts to share; messages of love, of warmth, of inspiration, of power. Many people keep this to themselves. The thought may be "I'm only one person, what difference can I make?" Oh, what a difference you can make!!! It need not matter if you have a group of 100, 000 hearing your words or only one. If you are moving just one person, you *are* making a difference! Share your words, share your life, share your light.

Don't let the light that lives inside you be hidden, don't let your gifts go unshared, throw light at the darkness. While you share your light with others, don't take that light for granted. Share your light with yourself; value yourself for all you are. Shine so bright, others will see you coming. They will welcome your presence, embrace you. Shine your light so bright that it's blinding. Shine your light for others, for yourself, for the world!

ABOUT THE AUTHOR

Harmony, energy and the divine beauty of the world are all channeled through the work of soulful Los Angeles-based entrepreneur, author, singer/songwriter, actress and musical mentor Oya Thomas. A life-long entrepreneur, Oya started her first company in high school. As she built her foundation as a creative artist, she developed a profound fascination for human psychology and the relationship between the mind, body, spirit, emotions and environment, which characterizes the core principles of both her mentoring and her musical repertoire. Her on-going quest to make her life and work a continuous opportunity for learning and growth drove her to earn a B.A. in Psychology at Loyola Marymount University and an M.A. in Spiritual Psychology at the University of Santa Monica, the country's leading institution in this discipline. Oya reaches the highest level of fulfillment as a singer, actress, life coach and mentor by watching the way her voice can move and shape the world around her and leading others to find their own sublime bliss and emotional freedom in the Arts. By combining her extensive spiritual and therapeutic training and her extremely multi-faceted artistic background, she has found an apt vehicle for her talents and is able to spread her light and love through one-on-one coaching as well as through her music and her commanding stage presence. Her album Spirit of Oya is available now. The 5 Star Points for Success: Manifest Your Dreams, Live Your Life's Purpose is her first book.